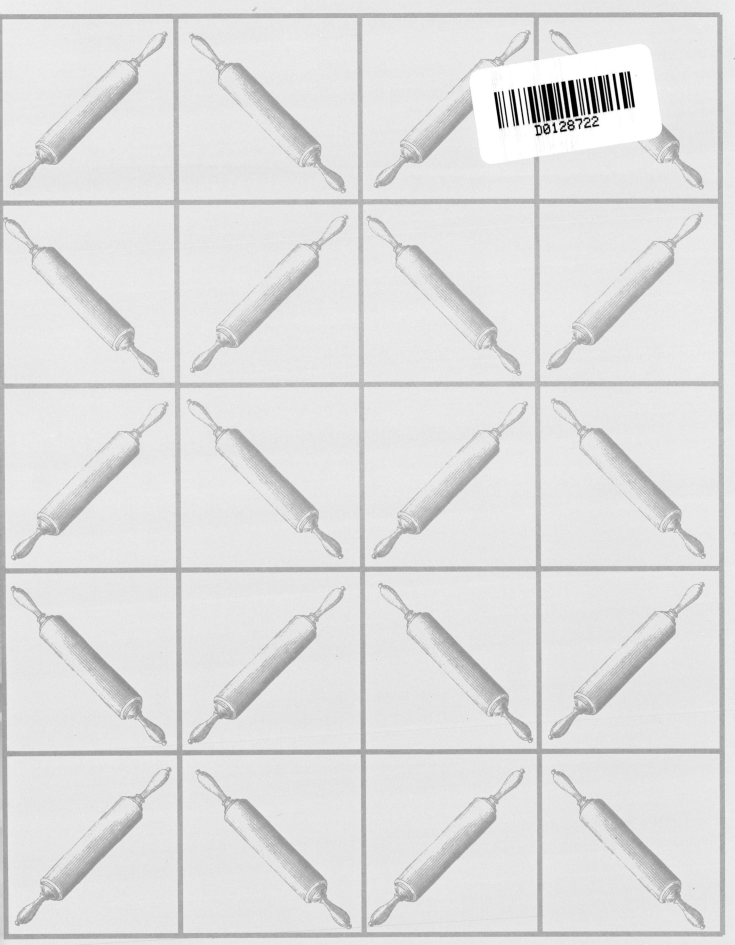

FAVORITE FOODS FROM THE OZARK WOODS

FAVORITE FOODS

from the
OZARK

WOODS

By
The Wood Family
Syble, Pauline, Marlene & Mona

Favorite Foods from the Ozark Woods Cookbook
Includes Index

Recipes - Wood Family and friends
Editor - Lori Jacobson
Editorial support - Cathey Forbes and Sandra Curiel Logan
Graphic design, production and food styling - Lori Jacobson
Photography - Shelle and Michael Neese, Studio 7, Albuquerque, NM
Photographic Assistant - Dougie Eckberg
Computer production - Phil Haxo and Shannon Cook
Title - Cathey Forbes
Printing and production - Staff and crew at Mitchell Web Press, San Diego, CA

Bella Vita Publishing
1022 Pueblo Solano N.W.
Albuquerque, New Mexico 87107

Manufactured and Printed in the United States of America

The country recipes in this book have been selected for their regional authenticity and most feature the
No Mess Dough Disc.

The ***No Mess Dough Disc*** is 16" in diameter and is made of light-weight, food grade, plastic. The disc has a removable fitted pastry cloth made of pre-shrunk 50 - 50 poly cotton fabric. A light dusting of flour on the fabric cover creates a perfect non-stick surface for rolling out almost any type of pastry, noodle or dumpling dough. After using the ***No Mess Dough Disc***, simply remove the cover and machine wash.

For more information on the ***No Mess Dough Disc*** call 1-800-456-0851

Favorite Foods of the Ozark Woods is lovingly dedicated to Ruby Wood, the most wonderful mother and grandmother any twelve children could have. All your kindness and love have paid off and we owe our success and happiness to you. Thank you for sharing your creative talents especially in the kitchen. Your delicious dumplings and raisin pie were the inspiration for this book.

Acknowledgement

A special acknowledgement to our husbands, Jim Whitlock, Wayne Dillard, David Wyatt, Curtis Elliott and our children, Michael, Rocky, Tina, Misty, Shane, Shawn, T.C. and Rebecca. Thank you for all your love, patience and support. We love you.

To our brothers and sisters: J.B. Wood, Earnestine Weaver, Norene Ply, L.B. Wood, Martha Dees, Bennie Mc Entire, Tammy Cantrall, Reda Sweet and L.D. Friend. Your moral support and encouragement has been an inspiration for us.

Cindy Gault, Barbara O'Dell, and the Arkansas Industrial Development Commission. Vernon Dewey, Judy Loving and Debbie Keeter. Forest and Nina Wood, Linda Hall, Gwen Stice, Linda Davenport, Chloe Richardson, Sharon Cole, all our employees and vendors. Most of all QVC Television; the staff and all the wonderful viewers who have purchased our product, you made this book possible!

A special note to our brother J.B. Wood.

J.B., we want you to know that we appreciate everything you did to make our lives better. All your hard work and sacrifice will never be forgotten. You have our unconditional love forever.

Preface

Living in a two room house in rural Marion County, Arkansas without modern conveniences would be hard for any size family, but it was a fact of life for the Wood family of twelve. Ben and Ruby Wood, parents of two boys and nine girls, graciously took in a cousin to even out the already large family. As you can imagine, creating three meals a day to satisfy this small army could be a challenge, yet Ruby managed quite well. With a lot of help from the children there was always a garden planted and water brought up from the spring. Hundreds of quarts of fresh fruits and vegetables were canned every summer so that even on the coldest winter day a fresh blackberry cobbler would be enjoyed. Did the children mind growing up under such conditions? The answer lies at Ruby's house where the family gathers every chance they can get; husbands, wives, children and grandchildren. Like most families the kitchen becomes a gathering place where gossip flies, stories are told and good food always takes the lead. As Ruby's family grows so do their appetites and their love. And that's how every recipe in this book was prepared; with the same love that surrounds Ruby's kitchen when her family comes together.

Country living contributed a wealth of knowledge and instilled an innovative spirit in the Wood family as witnessed by the success of the **No Mess Dough Disc**. Several years ago Marlene Wyatt, one of the younger Woods, created an easy way to make her family's favorite meal, chicken and dumplings. She covered a wooden disk with cotton sheeting from a pillowcase and stitched it with elastic to keep in place. Syble, one of her older sisters saw her invention and knew that this was an item that could be marketed to make kitchen life easier for everyone. Thanks to her sisters Syble Whitlock, Pauline Dillard and her niece Mona Elliott, Marlene was able to turn her idea into a marketable product. The four women pooled their resources and created Wood Family Enterprise. What started to be an easier and cleaner method for making dumpling and pie crust has become one of the most popular kitchen products on the market today and the Wood Family Enterprise has become a true American success story.

The **No Mess Dough Disc** is sold throughout the USA and Canada and on QVC Television. The recipes in this cookbook have been inspired by the Wood family and tested by Wood Family Enterprise. For the best results we recommend using the **No Mess Dough Disc** for recipes that require rolling dough and you too will appreciate the ease of creating delicious meals for your family.

HELPFUL HINTS

Every cook appreciates a short cut or new method for saving time and energy in the kitchen. The list below is is a compilation of proven tricks, techniques and substitutions that will improve your time in the kitchen.

SUGAR SUBSTITUTES

One cup of sugar can be substituted by the following equivalents.

Brown sugar 1/2 cup
Strained honey 3/4 cups
Molasses 1-1/2 cups
Corn syrup 2 cups
Maple syrup 1-1/2 cups

FLOUR EQUIVALENTS

One cup of sifted all purpose flour can be substituted by the following equivalents.

1 cup cake flour + 2 tablespoons flour
1/3 cup corn meal + 2/3 cups all purpose flour
1/2 cup corn meal + 1/2 all purpose flour
3/4 cups bran + 1/2 cup all puropse flour
1/2 cup bran + 1/2 cup all puropse flour
1/2 cup rice flour + 1/2 cup all purpose flour
1 cup rice flour
1/2 cup rye flour + 1/2 cup all pupose flour
1 cup rye flour
1/4 cup soybean flour + 3/4 cups all purpose flour
1/2 cup whole wheat + 1/2 cup all purpose flour
3/4 cups whole wheat flour + 1/4 cup all purpose flour

COOKING EQUIVALENTS

Take the guesswork out of cooking preparation.

1 lemon makes 3 tablespoons of juice.
1 lemon makes 1 teaspoon of grated peel.
1 orange makes 1/3 cup of juice.
1 orange makes 2 teaspoons grated peel.
1 pound of unshelled walnuts makes 1-1/2 to 1-3/4 cups shelled.
1 pound of unshelled almonds makes 3/4 cups to 1 cup shelled.
8 - 10 egg whites makes 1 cup.
12 - 14 egg yolks makes 1 cup.
1 pound of shredded American cheese makes 4 cups.
1 cup of unwhipped cream makes 2 cups whipped.
2 cups of butter=1 pound.
1 boullion cube=1 teaspoon beef extract.
1 tablespoon cornstarch =2/3 tablespoons arrowroot or
1-3/4 tablespoons wheat or rice flour.
1 tablespoon fresh horseradish=2 tablespoons bottled.
1 tablet rennet=1 tablespoon liquid rennet.
1-1/2 tablespoon quick cooking tapioca=1/4 cup pearl tapioca,
soaked 2 hours.

SUGAR EQUIVALENTS

1 pound berry or fruit sugar = 2-1/4 cups
1 pound brown sugar = 2 cups firmly packed
1 pound cane sugar = 1-1/2 cups
1 pound confectioners sugar = 2-1/2 cups
1 pound of corn syrup = 1-1/2 cups
1 pound of cube sugar = 180 - 220 pieces
1 pound of honey, strained = 1-1/2 cups
1 pound maple syrup = 1-1/2 cups

MEASUREMENT EQUIVALENTS

3 teaspoons = 1 tablespoon
2 tablespoons = 1/8 cup
4 tablespoons = 1/4 cup
8 tablespoons = 1/2 cup
16 tablespoons = 1 cup
5 tablespoons +1 teaspoon= 1/3 cup
12 tablespoons = 3/4 cups
4 ounces = 1/2 cup
8 ounces = 1 cup
16 ounces = 1 pound
1 ounce=2 tablespoons of fat or liquid
2 cups of fat = 1 pound
2 cups = 1 pint
2 cups sugar=1 pound
5/8 cups=1/2 cup + 2 tablespoons
7/8 cups = 3/4 cups +2 tablespoons
1 ounce of butter = 2 tablespoons
1 pound of butter = 4 sticks or 2 cups
2 pints = 1 quart
1 quart = 4 cups
A few grains = less than 1/8 teaspoon
Pinch = as much as can be taken between tip of finger and thumb
Dash or speck = less 1/8 teaspoon

ABBREVIATIONS

Cup = C.
Tablespoon = Tbsp.
Teaspoon = tsp.
Pound = lb.
Ounce = oz.
Package = pkg.
Gallon = gal.
Quart = qt.
Pint = pt.
Dozen = doz.
Large = lge.
Small = sm.

OVEN TEMPERATURES

All temperatures are quoted in fahrenheit degrees and may vary with individual ovens and altitude.

Temperature (F°)	Term
250 - 300	Slow
325	Moderately Slow
350	Moderate
375	Moderately Quick
400	Moderately hot
425 - 450	Hot
475 - 500	Extremely Hot

TIME TEMPERATURE AND TESTS

Baking times in pre-heated oven.

Baking Powder Biscuits	15 minutes
Bread	400° for 20 minutes,then 350° for 40 to 50 minutes
Coffee Bread	375° 25 minutes
Coffee Cake	400° 30 minutes
Cornbread	400° 30 minutes
Fruit or Nut Bread	350° 60 minutes
Muffins	425° 25 minutes
Popovers	400° 40 to 50 minutes
Rolls	400° 20 minutes
Spoonbread	350° 40 minutes
Dropped and Rolled Cookies	375° to 400° 10 to 12 minutes
Deep Dish Pies	450° for 10 minutes,then 350° 30 - 35 minutes
Meat Pies with Biscuit Top	450° 15 to 20 minutes
Meat Pies with Pastry Top	450° 15 minutes
Meringues on cooked filling	400° 1 to 2 minutes

TIPS FOR PERFECT PIES AND PASTRIES

To prevent an unbaked pie shell from puffing as it bakes, prick pastry thoroughly after placing in pie pan. Or, line the unbaked pastry shell with foil and fill with dry beans. Remove the beans and foil during the last 5 minutes of baking and allow to bake until golden brown.

Roll out pastry on light to heavily floured **No Mess Dough Disc** depending on the stickiness of the dough you are rolling. A good wooden ball bearing rolling pin is a must. The secret to keeping your rolling pin from getting sticky (and you do not need a rolling cover for pin) is always oil your rolling pin after each use, too much soap and water will dry out the wood. If you live in a humid climate store your rolling pin in the refrigerator.

For a pretty top crust, brush it with milk before baking or brush with water then sprinkle with sugar. Another alternative is to brush the top with beaten egg yolk or egg yolk mixed with water.

To measure for the perfect pie crust, shell place pie pan, open side down on rolled dough. Cut a circle 2 - 3 inches larger than the pie pan. Remove excess dough trimmings. Remove pie pan, fold dough round in half, then half again. Pick up and place in pie pan, unfolding to fill pan. To seal, fold and roll excess dough under, even with the pan rim and flute with desired technique.

Bake single shell pies at 375° - 400°, prick the bottom or line with foil and weight down with dry beans. Bake for 8 - 10 minutes.

Cover fluted edges with a 3 - 4 inch wide strip of aluminum foil to prevent browning; remove the foil during the last 15 minutes of baking.

MISCELLANEOUS KITCHEN HINTS

When cooking spaghetti or noodles, prevent boiling over by adding a few teaspoons of cooking oil.

Add a few drops of lemon juice to simmering rice, it will keep the grains separate.

To make catsup flow evenly out of the bottle, insert a drinking straw to the bottom of the bottle and remove.

If juice from an apple pie runs over in the oven, sprinkle salt on it; this will cause the juice to burn to a crisp and can be easily removed.

To prevent spattering when pan frying, sprinkle a little salt into the pan before adding fat.

Chill cheese for easier grating.

To keep cheese from drying out, wrap it in a cloth dampened with vinegar.

To determine whether an egg is fresh; immerse it in a pan of cool salted water. If the egg sinks, it is fresh, if it rises to the surface, throw it away.

To cut hard boiled eggs into smooth slices, dip the knife in hot water between slices.

Potatoes will bake faster if you boil them in salted water for 10 minutes, then wrap in foil and bake.

To make garlic butter, peel and slice a clove of garlic. Place in a bowl with 1/4 cup of butter. Cover tightly and let stand 30 to 60 minutes. Remove garlic.

To cleanse hands from vegetable stains, rub with a slice of raw potato or use a slice of lemon.

To remove odor from hands after peeling onions, rub some dry mustard on hands and wash in as usual.

When cooking cabbage place a small tin cup or can half full of vinegar on the stove near the cabbage. The vinegar will absorb the odor from the cooking cabbage.

MISCELLANEOUS KITCHEN HINTS

To keep scalding milk from scorching, rinse pan with hot water before using.

To prevent juices from cooking out of pies and into the oven, place a strip of pastry tape around the edge of pie; or place funnel or 4" stick or macaroni upright in center of pie.

To keep lemons fresh, place in a glass jar, fill with water and cover tightly.

To prevent annoying smoke when broiling; add a cup of water to the bottom portion of the broiling pan before sliding into oven.

To rid cutting boards of foul odors like fish, garlic and onions, cut a lemon or lime in half and rub surface of board.

Notes:_____

_____
_____
_____
_____
_____
_____
_____
_____
_____
_____
_____
_____
_____
_____
_____
_____
_____
_____
_____
_____
_____
_____
_____
_____
_____
_____
_____
_____

PIES

Center: Fresh Peach Pie. Top right to bottom: Chocolate Pie, Pecan Pie, Cherry Pie and Norene's Fried Pies.

Hot Water Pie Crust

Double this recipe and store in the refrigerator for up to one week. You'll be ready to bake a fresh pie in minutes.

1/4 cup boiling water
1/2 cup shortening
1 - 1/2 cups flour
1/2 teaspoon baking powder
1/2 teaspoon salt

Pour boiling water over shortening and mix until creamy. Mix in flour, baking powder and salt. Stir together to form a ball and chill. When ready to use, roll out to 1/8" thickness on lightly floured **No Mess Dough Disc.** This makes two - 9" pie shells.

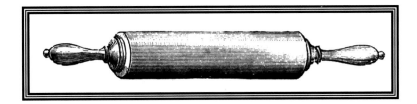

Rich Pastry

1-1/2 cups all purpose flour
1/2 teaspoon salt
1/4 cup vegetable shortening
1/4 cup (1/2 stick) butter or margarine
4 tablespoons cold water

Mix flour and salt, cut in shortening and butter until mixture is crumbly. Sprinkle with cold water, 1 tablespoon at a time. Mix until pastry holds together and leaves sides of bowl clean. Roll out on lightly floured **No Mess Dough Disc**. Fill and bake following instructions for the pie of your choice.

Pie Dough

A nice, flaky, easy to handle pie dough.

2-1/3 cups flour
1 teaspoon salt
1/2 cup plus 1 tablespoon salad oil
4 tablespoons water

With fork blend flour and salt. Add oil and mix well. Add 4 tablespoons of water and mix until completely moistened. (Adjust water as needed.) Roll out on lightly floured **No Mess Dough Disc** and use for your favorite pie shell or tarts.

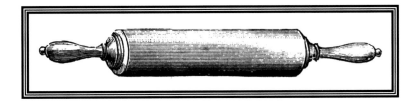

Baked Tart Shells

Use your favorite pie crust recipe.

Prepare pastry as directed, except roll into a 13" circle about 1/8" thick. Cut circle into 4-1/2"circles. Fit smaller circles over backs of medium muffin tins or 6 oz. custard cups, making pleats to conform closely to the the cups. Prick thoroughly with fork to prevent puffing. Heat oven to 375°. Place on un-greased cookie sheet. Bake until light brown (8 to 10 minutes). Cool before removing from pans. Fill each shell with 1/3 to 1/2 cup of favorite filling and garnish.

Step - by - Step Perfect Pie Crust

1. Mix ingredients until it resembles coarse meal.

4. Size dough by cutting a circle 1-1/2" larger than pan.

2. Shape dough into a round flat disc before rolling out.

5. Fold dough in half, then half again. Center and open.

3. Roll out to desired thickness.

6. Fold top crust over bottom and press to seal.

All step - by - step examples are prepared on the **No Mess Dough Disc.**

4

Step-by-Step Perfect Crust

Marlene and Pauline prepare a crust.

Fork Flute: Used tines of a fork to press into crust.

Rope Flute: Pinch between thumb and first knuckle.

Pinched Flute: Pinch and push with opposite finger.

Scallop Flute: Secure crust and pull with opposed fingers.

Lattice Crust: Woven strips of dough created this beauty.

Sugar Dough Pie Crust

2 sticks unsalted butter, softened
2-1/2 cups flour
1/3 cup sugar
1 egg
2 tablespoons vanilla

Combine butter, sugar and flour. Add egg and vanilla and mix until dough forms a ball. Place dough in plastic bag and chill for 30 minutes. Divide dough in half and roll out on lightly floured **No Mess Dough Disc.** Recipe makes 2 single pie crusts.

No Fail Pie Crust

3 cups all purpose flour
3/4 teaspoons salt
1 cup shortening
1 egg
1 teaspoon white vinegar
7 - 10 tablespoons cold water

Mix flour and salt, cut in shortening until texture of corn meal. In separate bowl mix egg, vinegar and water. Add dry ingredients and mix. Divide dough into thirds and roll out on lightly floured **No Mess Dough Disc** as needed. Yield: 3 single pie crusts.

Milky Pie Crust

4 cups flour
1-3/4 cups shortening
1 egg
1/2 cup milk
1 tablespoon vinegar
2 teaspoons sugar

Mix flour and sugar, cut in shortening until the texture of corn meal. Beat egg, milk and vinegar together and add to flour mixture. Work mixture until dough sticks together. Roll out on floured **No Mess Dough Disc.** Yield: 2, double crust pies.

Tips for Perfect Pies and Pastries

To cut in shortening evenly, use a pastry blender. If you don't have a pastry blender, use two knives in opposition, drawing back and forth, keeping the blades parallel.

Plain Pastry, Single Crust Pie

1-1/2 cups sifted all purpose flour
1 teaspoon salt
1/2 cup vegetable shortening
4 tablespoons cold water

Sift flour and salt together, cut in shortening until mixture is crumbly. Sprinkle with water, a tablespoon at a time; mix lightly with fork until pastry holds together and leaves sides of bowl clean. Roll out on lightly floured **No Mess Dough Disc.** Fill and bake according to recipe directions.

Plain Pastry, Double Crust Pie

2 cups sifted all purpose flour
1 teaspoon salt
2/3 cups vegetable shortening
4 - 6 tablespoons water

Follow same instructions as Plain Pastry, Single Crust Pie.

Skinny Pie Crust

If you're dieting and craving pie, make this crust. It has only half the calories of conventional crust.

1/2 cup sifted all purpose flour
1/4 teaspoon salt
1/4 teaspoon baking powder
1/4 cup diet margarine, softened

Sift flour, salt and baking powder into bowl. Cut in margarine until pastry leaves the sides of bowl. Shape into a ball; wrap in waxed paper, chill for 1 hour. Roll out on lightly floured **No Mess Dough Disc.** Fill and bake following recipe of your choice. Yield: 1 8" pie crust at 430 calories.

Nut Pie Shell

1-1/3 cups all purpose flour
1 teaspoon salt
1/4 cup pecans, finely chopped
1/3 cup oil
3 tablespoons cold milk

Mix flour, salt and nuts. Measure oil and milk together and pour into flour mixture. Stir until mixed. Roll out on lightly floured **No Mess Dough Disc,** place in a 9" pan. Prick with fork, bake at 450° for 5 minutes. Reduce heat to 350° and bake 10 minutes longer.

Best Yet Fruit Pie

Use strawberries, peaches or blackberries,

2 cups sugar
1/2 cup corn starch
1/2 teaspoon salt
2 cups water
1/2 cup corn syrup
1 teaspoon lemon juice
1 small box of fruit gelatin to match fruit selection
9" pie shell, baked

Mix sugar, cornstarch and salt. Add water, corn syrup and lemon juice. Bring to a boil and stir until thickened. Remove from heat, add fruit gelatin. Pour cooled mixture over fruit that has been arranged in cooked pie shell. Chill to set and serve with your favorite whipped topping.

Darn Good Pie

1-1/2 cups sugar
1 stick of butter or margarine
3 eggs
1 cup coconut
1 cup crushed pineapple, drained
9" pie shell, unbaked

Mix ingredients together and pour into pie shell. Bake at 375° for 35 - 40 minutes or until knife inserted comes out clean.

Tips For Perfect Pies and Pastries

Use proper bakeware. Choose heat - resistant glass pie plates or dull finish (anodized) aluminum pans. Never use shiny pans; pies will have a soggy crust.

Rhubarb Pie

Tangy rhubarb is delicious when accented with orange.

1-2/3 cups sugar
1/3 cup all purpose flour
1/2 teaspoon grated orange peel *(optional)
2 tablespoons butter or margarine
4 cups of rhubarb, cut into 1/2" pieces.

Heat oven to 425°. Prepare favorite pie crust. Mix sugar, flour and orange peel. Put half of the rhubarb into pastry lined pie pan. Sprinkle with half the sugar mixture. Repeat with remaining rhubarb and sugar mixture. Dot with butter or margarine. Cover with top crust, seal and flute edges and cut 4 - 5 slits in top crust. Sprinkle with sugar if desired. Bake at 425° for 40 - 50 minutes or until crust is brown.

Rhubarb Strawberry Pie

Use rhubarb pie recipe above:

Substitute strawberries for half the rhubarb and use 1-1/3 cups of sugar.

Raisin Pie

An all time Southern classic which can be made at any time of year.

3 eggs, separated
1 tablespoon butter
1 cup sugar
1 teaspoon sugar
1 teaspoon vinegar
1 teaspoon cinnamon
1 teaspoon cloves
1 teaspoon allspice
1/2 cup raisins, chopped
9"- pie shell, unbaked

Beat egg yolks slightly, add all other ingredients except egg whites. Beat whites until stiff and fold into mixture. Bake at 350° for 40 minutes. Serve with whipped cream.

Apple Pie

A year-round favorite that's sure to please dessert lovers everywhere.

9 Inch Pie

Pastry for 9" two crust pie (pages 6 & 7)
3/4 cups sugar
1/4 cup all purpose flour
1/2 teaspoon ground nutmeg
1/2 teaspoon ground cinnamon
1/8 teaspoon salt
6 cups thinly sliced, pared, tart apples
(about 6 medium apples)
2 tablespoons butter or margarine

10 Inch Pie

Pastry for 10" two crust pie (pages 6 & 7)
1 cup sugar
1/3 cup all purpose flour
1 teaspoon ground nutmeg
1 teaspoon ground cinnamon
1/8 teaspoon salt
8 cups thinly sliced, pared, tart apples
(about 7 medium apples)
3 tablespoons butter or margarine

Heat oven to 425°. Prepare pastry and line pie pan. Mix dry ingredients together. Stir in apples. Pour into pastry lined pie pan. Dot with butter or margarine. Cover with top crust, cut slits, seal and flute edges. Bake until crust is light brown and juice begins to bubble through slits in top. Approximately 40 - 50 minutes.

*Notes:*_____

_____
_____
_____
_____
_____
_____
_____
_____
_____
_____
_____
_____
_____
_____
_____
_____
_____
_____
_____
_____

Cherry Pie

9 Inch Pie

Pastry for 9", two - crust pie (pages 6 & 7)
1-1/3 cups sugar
1/3 cup all purpose flour
2 cans (16 oz. each) pitted red, tart cherries, drained
1/4 teaspoon almond extract
2 tablespoons butter or margarine

10 Inch Pie

Pastry for 10", two crust pie (pages 6 & 7)
1-2/3 cups sugar
1/2 cup all - purpose flour
3 cans (16 oz. each) pitted, red, tart cherries, drained
1 teaspoon almond extract
3 tablespoons butter or margarine

Heat oven to 425°. Prepare pastry and line desired pie pan. Mix sugar and flour. Stir in cherries. Pour cherry mixture into lined pie pan, sprinkle with almond extract. Dot with butter or margarine. Cover with top crust, cut slits in top, seal edges and flute. Bake until crust is light brown and juice begins to bubble through slits in crust. Approximately 35 - 45 minutes.

FRUIT PIZZA

Topping:

1-8 oz. package cream cheese
1/4 cup sugar
Fresh fruit, strawberries, peaches, bananas etc.

Mix cream cheese and sugar. Spread on cooled Sugar Dough Pie Crust (see page 6). Add fruit slices for topping.

Fresh Huckleberry Pie

If huckleberries are not available in your part of the country, substitute blueberries.

9" pie shell, baked
2 cups huckleberries
1/2 to 2/3 cups sugar (adjust to taste)
2/3 cups boiling water
2 tablespoons cornstarch
1-1/2 tablespoons lemon juice
2 tablespoons butter
1 cup whipping cream
1/8 teaspoon salt

Mix together sugar, salt and cornstarch. Gradually add boiling water, stirring constantly. Add one cup of berries, cook until thick and clear. Add lemon juice and butter. Cool to lukewarm. Add second cup of berries. Chill about 2 hours before serving. Add 2 tablespoons sugar to whipping cream and beat until stiff. Spoon cream into cooled pie shell, piling high around edges. Spoon berry sauce into whipped cream. Chill until serving time.

Peach Pie

9" baked pie shell
Boil until thick and clear:
4 mashed peaches
1 cup sugar
2 tablespoons lemon juice
3 tablespoons cornstarch

If peaches are very juicy, add more cornstarch. Pour mixture into baked pie shell. Let cool and slice 4 fresh peaches into pie. Keep refrigerated until serving time. Top with whipped cream, ice-cream or your favorite creamy topping.

Easy Apple Turnovers

Roll out Never - Fail Pie Crust pie crust recipe (page 6) one half at a time, on lightly floured **No Mess Dough Disc**. Cut out 12 rounds, 1/4" thick with a 4" cookie cutter or biscuit cutter.

Filling:

1 can (1 lb. 4 oz.) pie sliced apples, drained
3 tablespoons brown sugar
1/2 teaspoon ground allspice
vegetable oil for frying
powdered sugar

Toss apples with brown sugar and allspice. Spread 2 tablespoons apple mixture over half of each pastry round. Fold other half over filling. Press edges with fork to seal. Drop turnovers, a few at a time, in 1" very hot oil. Fry, turning often for 3 - 5 minutes or until golden. Remove from oil, drain and blot with paper towels. While warm, sprinkle with powdered sugar, serve slightly warm. Yield: One dozen.

Millionaire Pie

Tastes as rich as the name implies!

9" pie crust, baked
1 cup powdered sugar, sifted
1/4 cup powdered sugar, sifted
1/2 stick butter, softened
1 egg
1/8 teaspoon salt
1/8 teaspoon vanilla
1/2 cup heavy cream
1/2 cup crushed pineapple, drained
1/4 cup chopped pecans

Cream butter and 1 cup powdered sugar with mixer. Add egg, salt and vanilla, beat until light and fluffy. Spread in pie shell and chill until set. Beat heavy cream until stiff. Blend in 1/4 cup powdered sugar. Fold in pineapple and pecans. Top pie and chill.

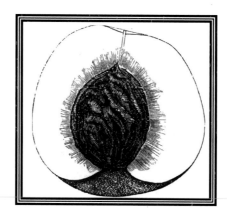

Peach Tart

9" baked pie shell, cooled
1- (4 oz.) package instant vanilla pudding mix
1 cup milk
1- (8 oz.) carton dairy sour cream
1/4 teaspoon almond extract
1-(1 lb., 14 oz.) canned cling peach slices
1 tablespoon cornstarch
1 tablespoon lemon juice
1/4 cup flaked coconut

Combine pudding mix with milk, sour cream and almond extract. Prepare following label instructions. Pour into cooled crust. Let stand 5 minutes or until filling is set. Drain syrup from peaches. (save) Arrange peach slices, slightly overlapping on top of filling. Slowly blend 2/3 cup of the peach syrup mixture with cornstarch. Cook until mixture thickens and bubbles, about 1 minute. Stir in lemon juice. Cool slightly, spoon over peaches to glaze. Chill, garnish with coconut before serving.

Fresh Strawberry Pie

9" pie crust, baked and cooled
2 cups sugar
2 cups water
1/4 teaspoon salt
8 tablespoons cornstarch
1/3 cup white corn syrup
1 quart of whole strawberries
1 box strawberry gelatin
whipped topping

Boil suger, water, salt, cornstarch and corn syrup until they become thick and clear. Pour gelatin over berries; add a few drops of red food coloring if desired. After liquid has cooled, pour over berries. Pour into baked pie shell. Top with whipped topping. Refrigerate for 2 - 3 hours before serving.

Mystery Pecan Pie

9" unbaked pie shell
1 - 8 oz. package cream cheese
1 egg
1/3 cup sugar
1 teaspoon vanilla
1-1/4 cups coarsely chopped pecans
3 eggs
1/4 teaspoon salt
1 teaspoon vanilla
1 cup corn syrup
1/4 cup sugar

Cream together cheese, 1 egg, 1/3 cup sugar and 1 teaspoon vanilla. Beat until fluffy. Spread on bottom of pie shell. Sprinkle pecans over cream cheese. Beat eggs until fluffy, add salt, vanilla, corn syrup and sugar. Mix well, pour over pecans. Bake at 375° for 35 to 40 minutes.

Chocolate Pie

9" baked pie shell
1/4 cup cocoa
1/4 cup flour
1 cup sugar
1/2 teaspoon salt
2 cups milk
2 egg yolks
3 tablespoons butter
1 teaspoon vanilla

Cook cocoa, flour, sugar, salt and milk until thick. Beat egg yolks, butter and vanilla; add to cooked mixture. Pour into baked pie shell and let cool. Top with meringue or serve with whipped cream. If served with whipped cream, use the whole egg in filling.

Granny Ruby's Raisin Pie

2 cups of water
2 cups raisins
1 teaspoon cinnamon
1 teaspoon pumpkin pie spice
1 teaspoon vanilla
1 cup sugar
5 teaspoons plain flour
1/2 cup water

Mix first two ingredients together and cook over low heat until tender. Add spices, vanilla and sugar. Bring to a boil. Stir flour and water together. Add to hot mixture. Stir until thickened. Pour into pastry - lined pan. Adjust top crust. Flute edges. Bake at 400° for about 40 minutes.

French Meringue

2 egg whites, beaten
2 cups sugar
3/4 cups water
1 teaspoon vanilla

Heat sugar and water, stirring until sugar is dissolved. Continue cooking without stirring until temperature reaches 238°F or syrup forms a soft ball when tested in cold water. Remove from heat and pour slowly into stiffly beaten egg whites beating constantly. Continue beating until mixture is cool. Add flavoring. Shape meringue into a ring with spoon or pipe with pastry tube onto a moist board covered with brown paper. Bake at 270° for 1 hour. Yield: 10 to 12 shells.

Brown Sugar Meringue

2 egg whites
4 tablespoons brown sugar
1/2 teaspoon vanilla

Beat egg whites until fluffy. Add sugar, gradually beat until stiff. Add vanilla and pile onto pie, sealing edges. Bake at 325° - 350° until golden brown. Yield: Topping for a 9" pie.

Marshmallow Meringue

1/2 pound of marshmallows
1 tablespoon milk
2 egg whites
1/4 cup sugar
1/4 teaspoon salt
1/2 teaspoon vanilla

Heat marshmallows and milk together, folding until half melted. Remove from heat and continue folding until mixture is smooth and fluffy. Beat egg whites add, sugar and continue beating until stiff and smooth. Add salt and vanilla, blend into marshmallow mixture and spread over pie. Bake at 450° or 1 minute or until golden brown.

Peach Cobbler with Biscuits

9" x 13" baking pan, buttered

Fruit:

6 cups peeled, pitted and sliced peaches
1/2 cup pitted sour cherries or raspberries
4 tablespoons flour
1-1/2 cups sugar
1/8 teaspoon cinnamon or nutmeg
Juice of 1/2 fresh lemon

Biscuits:

2 cups flour
2 tablespoons sugar
3 teaspoons baking powder
1 teaspoon salt
1 teaspoon baking soda
4 tablespoons butter
3/4 cups plain yogurt
1/4 cup heavy cream

Preheat oven to 425°. Toss the fruit with flour, sugar, spices and lemon juice. Pour into buttered baking dish. Sift flour, sugar, baking powder, salt and baking soda together. Cut in butter until mixture resembles coarse meal. Stir in yogurt and cream. Knead gently on lightly floured, **No Mess Dough Disc**. Pat out to 1/2" thickness and cut into 10 individual rounds. Place the biscuit rounds on top of fruit. Cut the dough scraps into triangles and fill in between rounds. Bake at 425° about 25 minutes. Serve with whipped cream.

Buttermilk Pie

9" pie shell, unbaked
3 eggs, slightly beaten
1 cup sugar
1/2 cup butter, melted and cooled
2 tablespoons plain flour
1 teaspoon vanilla
2 cups buttermilk
ground nutmeg

Pre-bake crust for 4 - 5 minutes at 450°. Blend eggs, sugar, butter, flour and vanilla. Slowly add buttermilk and pour into pie shell. Sprinkle with nutmeg and bake until knife inserted in middle of pie comes out clean, about 35 - 45 minutes.

Magic Lemon Meringue Pie

9" pie shell, baked

Filling

1 can sweetened condensed milk
1/2 cup lemon juice
1 teaspoon grated lemon rind
2 egg yolks

Combine milk, lemon juice and lemon rind. Blend in egg yolks. Pour into cooled crust. Top with meringue.

Meringue

2 egg whites
1/4 teaspoon cream of tartar
1/4 cup sugar

Beat egg whites and cream of tartar until soft peaks form. Gradually add sugar and beat until stiff peaks are formed. Spread over filling, sealing to edge of crust. Bake at 325° for 12 - 15 minutes.

Banana Cream Pie

9" pie shell, baked
2/3 cups sugar
1/4 cup cornstarch
1/2 teaspoon salt
3 cups milk
4 egg yolks, slightly beaten
2 tablespoons margarine or butter, softened
1 tablespoon plus 1 teaspoon vanilla
2 - 3 large bananas, sliced

Mix sugar, cornstarch and salt in saucepan. Gradually stir in milk. Stir in beaten egg yolks. Cook over medium heat, stirring constantly until mixture thickens and boils. Boil and stir 1 minute. Remove from heat, stir in butter or margarine and vanilla. Press plastic wrap onto filling and allow to cool. Place sliced bananas in pie shell, pour cooled filling over bananas. Top with whipped cream.

Coconut Cream Pie

Follow instructions for Banana Cream Pie except decrease vanilla to 2 teaspoons and add 1 cup of flaked coconut after removing from heat. Omit bananas.

Sour Cream Walnut Pie

1/2 cup butter
1/2 cup brown sugar
3/4 cups sugar
4 eggs beaten
1/2 teaspoon salt
1/2 cup sour cream
1/4 cup light corn syrup
1/4 teaspoon lemon extract
1 teaspoon vanilla extract
1-1/2 cups walnuts, chopped

Combine butter, sugars, eggs, salt, sour cream and corn syrup in saucepan. Mix well and heat on low, stirring until well blended, about 5 minutes. Remove from heat and add lemon and vanilla extract and nuts. Pour into pie shell and bake at 350° for 1 hour or until center is set.

Sour Cream Raisin Pie

9" pie shell, baked
1 cup raisins
3-1/2 cups water
1 cup sugar
3 egg yolks
Juice of 1 lemon
3 tablespoons flour
12 ounces sour cream
1/8 teaspoon salt
1/2 stick butter, melted
3 tablespoons warm water
whipped cream

Cover raisins with water and cook for 35 minutes. Add sugar. Mix flour, salt, egg yolks and lemon juice with warm water. Add mixture to raisins. Fold in sour cream and butter. Return mixture to heat and cook until it thickens. Cool filling and pour into pie crust. Top with whipped cream.

Pecan Pie

9" pie shell, unbaked
3 eggs, slightly beaten
1 cup corn syrup, either light or dark
1 cup sugar
2 tablespoons butter, softened
1 tablespoon vanilla
1-1/2 cups pecans

In a large bowl combine eggs, syrup, sugar, butter and vanilla. Stir until well blended. Add pecans. Pour into pie shell and bake at 350° for 50 - 55 minutes. Cool before serving.

Low Calorie Pumpkin Pie

Even dieters can enjoy this delicious pie, it's only 120 calories per slice!

Skinny Pie Crust, unbaked (page 7)
1 cup pumpkin
2 eggs
1-1/4 cups skim milk
1/4 cup packed brown sugar
granulated or liquid sweetener
1/2 teaspoon cornstarch
1/4 teaspoon salt
1/2 teaspoon ground cinnamon
1/8 teaspoon each, ground allspice, ginger and nutmeg

Combine pumpkin, eggs, milk, brown sugar, no calorie sweetener to equal 12 teaspoons sugar, cornstarch, salt and spices until smooth and creamy. Pour into prepared, uncooked pie shell. Bake at 350° for 1 hour or until crust is lightly browned and filling is set.

Pumpkin Pie

8" pie shell, unbaked
1 cup canned pumpkin
1/2 teaspoon cinnamon
1/4 teaspoon ginger
1/4 teaspoon nutmeg
1/8 teaspoon cloves
1 cup milk, half & half or evaporated milk
1/2 cup sugar
1 egg, slightly beaten
1/2 teaspoon salt

Blend pumpkin and spices thoroughly. Stir in remaining ingredients; mix well. Pour into pastry shell and bake at 400° for about 1 hour. Pie is done when knife inserted in center comes out clean.

BREADS, BISCUITS & SWEET ROLLS

Top left: Italian Braid, Cloverleaf Rolls, Jam Whirl Pinwheel, Best - Ever Cinnamon Rolls, No - Fail Biscuits, 3 - Grain Bread

Butterhorn Rolls

1 cup milk
1/2 cup sugar
1 teaspoon salt
1/2 cup butter, melted
2 packages yeast
1/4 cup warm water
3 eggs, beaten
4-1/2 cups flour

Scald milk and cool to lukewarm. Add yeast which has been dissolved in water, eggs, sugar and salt. Mix until blended. Stir in flour. Combine well, let rise until double in bulk, about two hours. Turn out on well floured **No Mess Dough Disc** and divide into four parts. Dough will be moist. Roll each section as for pie crust and brush with melted butter. Cut each section into twelve wedge shaped pieces. Roll each wedge from the wide end. Put on lightly greased cookie sheet and brush tops with melted butter. Let rise until light. Bake at 375° for 15 minutes.

Sweet Potato Rolls

A delicious twist on a classic biscuit recipe. The beautiful rich color and sweet taste of these rolls make them a perfect addition to any pork, chicken, turkey or wild game meals. They're also terrific with jam, honey or syrup for tea time!

2 packages yeast
4 tablespoons sugar
1/2 cup warm water
3 tablespoons butter, melted
1 tablespoon salt
3 eggs
3-1/2 cups - 4 cups flour
1/2 cup mashed sweet potatoes
2 tablespoons cream

Combine the yeast with 1 tablespoon of sugar and warm water. Cover and put in a warm place until the mixture doubles in bulk. Add the remaining sugar, butter, salt and 2 eggs to the yeast mixture. Stir until well blended. Stir in flour, 1 cup at a time, then add sweet potatoes. Place on a lightly floured **No Mess Dough Disc** and knead until the dough is smooth and elastic. Allow to rise about 1 hour. Punch the dough down and shape into a ball. Pinch off 3 large marble size balls of dough and place in greased muffin tins. Let rise again. Beat the remaining egg with cream and brush the tops of rolls. Bake at 375° for 20 minutes. Yield: 2 dozen rolls.

No Fail Crescent Rolls

1 package yeast
1-1/4 cups lukewarm water
1/4 cup sugar
1 teaspoon salt
3 eggs, well beaten
3/4 cups melted butter or vegetable oil
4 cups all purpose flour

Dissolve yeast in water, add sugar, salt, eggs, butter (or oil) and flour. Stir until smooth. Dough will be sticky. Cover tightly and put in refrigerator until ready to use. Dough will keep four to five days. When ready to use, roll out on floured **No Mess Dough Disc** to 1/2" in thickness. Cut dough in 6" triangles and roll from large side to small to form a crescent shape. Let rise for 1 hour or until double in size. Bake 350° for 10 - 15 minutes. Yield: Two dozen rolls.

Super Simple Sweet Rolls

1 cup shortening
1 cup boiling water
1 cup cold water
3 eggs, beaten
3/4 cups white sugar
2 teaspoons salt
3 packages yeast
1/2 cup warm water
8 - 9 cups white flour
1/2 cup butter, softened
1 cup brown sugar
1/2 teaspoon cinnamon
raisins and/or nuts

Melt shortening in boiling water, add cold water to cool. Mix eggs, sugar and salt. Dissolve yeast in warm water and add to mixture, stir. Add flour to make dough. Knead on lightly floured **No Mess Dough Disc**, adding flour until no longer sticky. Divide dough in half. Roll each half into large rectangle and cover with 1/4 cup softened butter, 1/2 cup brown sugar, 1/4 teaspoon cinnamon and optional raisins or nuts. Roll up jellyroll style and cut into 1" thick slices. Place, cut side down in two greased 9" x 13" pans. Let rise until double in bulk. Bake at 350° for 30 - 35 minutes.

Step - by - Step Basic Yeast Dough & Jellyroll Technique

1. Dough should rise to double in bulk.

1. Spread rolled dough with butter then add spices, sugars or fruit, jams, jellies or preserves.

2. Punch down to let gasses escape.

2. Roll dough tightly, lengthwise to form a long, slender cylinder.

3. Knead the dough to create elasticity.

3. Cut the jellyroll into 1" -1-1/2" slices using dental floss or strong thread.

Simple Cinnamon Twist

2 tablespoons butter
1/4 cup sugar
1 teaspoon cinnamon
1 package refrigerator biscuits

Preheat oven to 425°. Melt butter in small pan. Combine sugar and cinnamon in small bowl. Roll each biscuit into a 9" rope on lightly floured **No Mess Dough Disc.** Twist each rope to form a figure 8. Pinch end together to seal. Dip the biscuits in melted butter then in cinnamon sugar. Place on baking sheet. Bake at 425° for 5 - 8 minutes.

Chocolate Sticky Rolls

Dough

2 cups (1 pound) frozen bread dough
(thawed according to packaged directions)

Caramel:

3/4 cups firmly packed brown sugar
1/4 cup butter, melted
2 tablespoons semi - sweet chocolate chips
2 tablespoons light corn syrup

Filling:

3/4 cups semi - sweet chocolate chips
1/4 teaspoon cinnamon
3 tablespoons milk
1/2 cup chopped pecans

In medium bowl, stir together all caramel ingredients. Spread caramel on bottom of greased 9" x 13" baking pan. In 1 quart saucepan combine all filling ingredients except pecans and bread dough. Cook over low heat, stirring occasionally, until chocolate chips are melted. On lightly floured **No Mess Dough Disc** roll each loaf of bread dough into a 10" x 14" rectangle. Spread half of filling (about 1/4 cup) on each dough rectangle; sprinkle each half with 1/4 cup pecans. Roll each rectangle into a tight roll, starting with the 14" side. Pinch edges of dough to seal roll. Cut into 8 slices. Place dough slices in greased pan, cover and allow to rise until double in bulk. Bake at 375° for 25 - 30 minutes or until golden brown. Yield: 16 rolls.

Basic Sweet Yeast Dough

2 packages yeast
1/2 cup warm water
1 teaspoon salt
1 cup milk
1/2 cup sugar
2 eggs
1/4 cup shortening
5 cups flour
1 teaspoon grated lemon rind

Preheat oven to 350°. Dissolve yeast in warm water. Scald milk; add sugar, salt and shortening. Cool to lukewarm. Add flour to make a thick batter; mix well. Add yeast, eggs, and lemon rind; beat well, add more flour to make a soft dough. Knead on lightly floured *No Mess Dough Disc* until smooth. Place in greased bowl, turn to coat, cover, let rest 10 minutes. Shape into rolls. Let rise until double in bulk. Bake at 350° for 15 - 20 minutes. Yield: 2-1/2 dozen rolls.

Dessert Shortcake

1-3/4 cups unsifted, plain flour
3 teaspoons baking powder
3/4 teaspoons salt
1/4 cup sugar
1/2 cup shortening
1/4 cup milk
1 egg, well beaten

Mix flour, baking powder, salt and sugar together. Cut in shortening, until mixture resembles coarse meal, using pastry blender or fork. Add milk and egg. Stir with fork until soft dough is formed. Knead on lightly floured *No Mess Dough Disc* about 30 seconds. Roll to 1/4" thickness. Cut with floured 3" cutter. Place half the circles on baking sheet; brush with melted butter. Place remaining circles on top; brush with butter. Bake at 425° for 10 -12 minutes.

To serve:

Separate warm shortcakes, butter and fill with fruit and whipped cream.

Jam Whirl Pinwheel

2-1/2 cups flour
3 teaspoons baking powder
1 teaspoon salt
1/2 cup shortening
1 egg, slightly beaten
1/3 cup milk
1/2 cup raspberry jam (or any flavor desired)
1 cup sifted confectioners sugar
2 tablespoons milk

Sift together flour, baking powder and salt. Cut in shortening. Combine the egg and milk and add to flour mixture. Stir until soft dough is formed. Knead on lightly floured **No Mess Dough Disc** about 30 seconds. Roll into oblong sheet, 1/8" in thickness. Spread dough with jam. Roll tightly from wide end and seal edges. Bring ends together to form a ring. Place on greased baking sheet. With scissors, cut 1" slices into ring, but not through. Turn slices, cut side up. Brush with melted butter. Bake at 400° for 20 - 25 minutes. Combine sugar and milk to make glaze and spread over hot ring. Serve warm.

Chocolate Chip Scones

1-3/4 cups all purpose flour
3 tablespoons sugar
2-1/2 teaspoons baking powder
1/2 teaspoon salt
1/3 cup butter
1 egg, slightly beaten
1/2 cup semi - sweet chocolate chips
4 - 6 tablespoons half and half
1 egg, slightly beaten

In medium bowl combine flour, sugar, baking powder and salt. Cut butter into flour mixture until it resembles fine crumbs. Stir in egg, chocolate chips and enough half and half so dough leaves sides of bowl. Knead dough on lightly floured **No Mess Dough Disc.** Roll to 1/2" thick circle. Cut into 12 wedges. Place on cookie sheet. Brush with beaten egg. Bake at 400° for 10 - 12 minutes.

Maple Cinnamon Bundles

3 cups flour, sifted
2 tablespoons sugar
6 teaspoons baking powder
1 teaspoon salt
1/2 cup shortening
1 egg
3/4 cup cold water
4 teaspoons butter, softened
2/3 cups seedless raisins
grated maple sugar
cinnamon
caramel syrup

Sift together flour, sugar, baking powder and salt. With pastry knife, cut shortening into flour. Beat egg in cup adding 3/4 cup water to make 1 cup. Add egg mixture to flour and mix. Knead on lightly floured **No Mess Dough Disc** until smooth. Roll out to 1/2" thick rectangle. Spread with softened butter, sprinkle with raisins, grated maple sugar and cinnamon. Roll up tightly from wide end. Cut in pieces 2" thick. Dip in caramel syrup place in greased baking pan. Bake at 400° about 30 minutes. Remove from oven, invert pan immediately onto serving plate.

Caramel Syrup:

4 tablespoons butter
1/2 cup corn syrup

Melt butter in heavy skillet, add corn syrup and cook till blended.

Cinnamon Coffee Cake Ring

1 package yeast
1/4 cup warm water
1/4 cup shortening
1 egg
1 teaspoon salt
1/4 cup sugar
3/4 cups lukewarm milk, scalded then cooled
3-1/2 cups flour (add 1/4 cup more if needed)
2 tablespoons butter, softened
1/2 cup sugar
2 teaspoons cinnamon
1 cup nuts, chopped

Frosting:

1 cup powdered sugar
1 tablespoon vanilla
1 tablespoon warm milk

Dissolve yeast in warm water. Cream shortening, add egg, salt and sugar mix well. Slowly add dissolved yeast. Continue mixing and slowly adding the milk. Add flour, 1 cup at a time, mixing well after each addition. Knead dough on lightly floured **No Mess Dough Disc** until smooth and elastic. Cover and let rise until double in bulk. Punch down and let rise until double, about 30 minutes. Roll dough on lightly floured **No Mess Dough Disc** to 1/2" in thickness. Spread with butter and sprinkle with cinnamon and sugar. Sprinkle with chopped nuts and roll up tightly, lengthwise and pinch to seal edges. Place on greased baking sheet, seam side down and shape into a ring. With scissors cut 2/3 into ring at 1" intervals pull each section apart as you cut. Let rise until double in bulk, about 35 - 40 minutes. Bake at 375° for 25 - 30 minutes. Combine frosting ingredients, mix well and frost coffee cake while warm.

Caramel or Pecan Rolls

1 pkg. of yeast
3/4 cup warm water
1/2 teaspoon salt
5 tablespoons sugar
6 cups flour
2 cups scalded milk
2 eggs, well beaten

Filling:
(for each section of dough)
4 tablespoons sugar
4 tablespoons butter, softened
1-1/2 teaspoons cinnamon (omit for caramel rolls)
1/4 cup broken pecans

Topping
3 tablespoons melted butter
Brown sugar
Pecan halves

Scald milk and set aside to cool to lukewarm. Add yeast to warm water and set aside to soften. Mix together dry ingredients, adding lukewarm milk, eggs and softened yeast. Stir until dough is smooth. Place in greased bowl, turn to coat, cover and let rise until double in bulk. Place dough on well floured **No Mess Dough Disc**. Let rest for 10 minutes. Knead dough until smooth and elastic adding flour as needed. Divide dough into 2 to 3 equal sections. Roll out each section on a lightly floured **No Mess Dough Disc** to a rectangle 1/2" in thickness. To prepare filling, cream together softened butter, sugar and cinnamon. Spread over rolled-out dough. Sprinkle with pecans. Roll up lengthwise, pinch and seal edges. For topping, melt butter in baking pan, add brown sugar to the depth of 1/4". Press pecan halves into sugar. Cut roll into slices 3/4" thick. Place cut side down in pan. Cover and let rise until double in bulk. Bake at 375° for 25 minutes. Yield: 24 rolls.

Variations:

Add 1 cup raisins to filling and top with brown sugar. Omit cinnamon for caramel rolls. If so desired, dough can be refrigerated overnight.

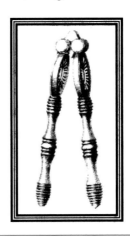

Holiday Fruit Bundles

3-ounces cream cheese, softened
2 tablespoons brown sugar
1/8 teaspoon cinnamon
1/8 teaspoon almond extract
1/3 cup candied fruit, diced
1/4 cup raisins
1/4 cup nuts
candied cherries (optional)
No - Fail Piecrust (pg. 6) or your favorite pastry

Glaze:

1 cup powdered sugar, sifted
1-1/2 tablespoons milk
3-4 drops almond extract

Mix cream cheese, brown sugar, cinnamon and almond extract. Add candied fruit, raisins and nuts. Roll out pastry on lightly floured **No Mess Dough Disc.** Cut into 4 rectangles, cut again to make 2 squares from each rectangle. Place 1 tablespoon of candied fruit mixture in center of each square. Shape into a ball and place seam side down on ungreased cookie sheet. Bake at 350° for 15 - 20 minutes or until browned. Cool slightly, drizzle glaze over each roll and decorate with candied cherries.

Easy Strudel

1/2 pound margarine
2 cups flour
3 egg yolks
2 tablespoons vinegar
1/4 cup water

Cut margarine into flour; add egg yolks, vinegar and water. Mix well, cover and refrigerate overnight. Divide dough into thirds; roll each section out on lightly floured **No Mess Dough Disc** to 10" x 15" rectangle.

Strudel Filling:

3 tablespoons flour
9 tablespoons sugar
1-1/2 teaspoons cinnamon
9 apples peeled and diced

Mix 1 tablespoon flour, 3 tablespoons sugar and 1/2 teaspoon cinnamon for each rectangle. Sprinkle over top. Arrange 3 apples along edge of long side; roll up. Place on greased pan. Bake at 375 ° for 45 minutes.

Orange Tea Ring

2 packages dry yeast or 2 cakes
1/2 cup warm water
3/4 cups lukewarm milk
1/3 cup sugar
1/2 cup shortening
2 eggs
1/4 cup orange juice
2 tablespoons orange rind
5 cups sifted all purpose flour
1/2 teaspoon salt
soft butter

Soak yeast in warm water for 5 minutes. Combine milk with sugar and salt. Stir to dissolve. Beat in shortening, eggs, orange juice, rind, 1 cup flour and yeast mixture, beat until smooth. Add remaining flour until dough leaves sides of bowl. Knead dough on lightly floured **No Mess Dough Disc** until it becomes smooth and no longer sticky. Divide dough in 2 parts. Roll into rectangle 1/4" thick and spread with soft butter. Roll up tightly from long side. Pinch edges to seal. Place sealed edge down on greased baking sheet. Bring ends together to form a ring, pinch edges together to seal. Cut with scissors 2/3 into ring at 1" intervals. Turn each section and twist to expose cut surface. Let rise until double in bulk. Bake at 375° for 25 - 30 minutes.

Glaze:

2 cups powdered sugar
3 tablespoons orange juice
2 teaspoons grated orange rind.

Combine sugar, juice and rind. Brush on ring.

Old - Fashioned Buttermilk Biscuits

2 cups buttermilk
2 tablespoons sugar
1 teaspoon baking soda
1 cup shortening
5-1/2 cups self - rising flour
1 package yeast
1/4 cup warm water

Preheat oven to 350°. Combine buttermilk, sugar and baking soda. In a large bowl cut shortening into 4 cups of flour until it resembles the texture of small peas. Dissolve the yeast in warm water. Add the buttermilk and yeast mixture to the flour and mix well. Turn out on well floured **No Mess Dough Disc,** add more flour to top. Knead dough, adding flour until no longer sticky. Roll out to 1" in thickness and cut with biscuit cutter. Place on non-stick baking pan or spray with non-stick spray. Bake at 400° for 25 minutes or until lightly browned. Yield: 4 dozen biscuits.

Hostess Tea Biscuits

1-3/4 cups sifted all purpose flour
3/4 teaspoons salt
3 teaspoons baking powder
1/3 cup shortening
3/4 cups milk
2 teaspoons orange rind

Mix flour, baking powder and salt together. Cut in shortening and orange rind. Mixture will look like coarse corn meal. Add milk, stir with fork until soft dough is formed. Knead on lightly floured **No Mess Dough Disc**. Roll out to 1/2" in thickness. Cut with biscuit cutter and place on ungreased baking sheet. Spread tops with glaze. Bake at 450° for 10 - 12 minutes.

Glaze:

1 tablespoon sugar
1-1/2 teaspoons orange juice

Mix together and spread on top of unbaked biscuits.

Tips for Perfect Yeast Doughs and Biscuits

If doughs are too sticky to work with gradually add more flour until smooth.

Angel Biscuits

Our angel biscuits are as heavenly as the name suggests. The dough will keep in the refrigerator for several weeks. Just cut, let rise for twenty to thirty minutes and bake as directed.

1 package of yeast
1/2 cup warm water
5 cups all purpose flour
1 teaspoon baking soda
1 teaspoon salt
3 tablespoons sugar
3/4 cups vegetable shortening
2 cups buttermilk

Dissolve yeast in water. Sift dry ingredients together. Cut in shortening, add buttermilk and dissolved yeast. Stir together until all the flour is moistened. Cover bowl and put in refrigerator until ready to use. When ready, take out as much as needed. Roll out on **No Mess Dough Disc** to 1/2" thickness and cut with biscuit cutter. Bake in pre-heated 400° oven on slightly greased cookie sheet for about 12 minutes.

Easy Dough's It Yeast Rolls

1 package yeast
1/2 cup warm water
1 egg
1/2 cup milk
1 tablespoon sugar
1/2 stick margarine, melted
3-1/2 cups biscuit mix

Dissolve yeast in water. Mix egg, milk, sugar and margarine. Add yeast and mix well. Stir in biscuit mix and blend until smooth. Pour into buttered bowl. Cover and let rise until doubled in bulk, about one hour. Turn dough out onto **No Mess Dough Disc** floured with biscuit mix. Work mix into dough until it is elastic and not sticky. Roll out to 1" in thickness and cut with cutter. Fold each roll in half and put into greased pan with sides slightly touching. Let rise for 30 - 45 minutes. Bake at 350° for 15 - 20 minutes.

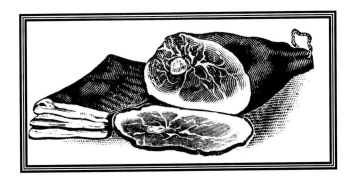

Bacon & Cheese Biscuits

2 cups self - rising flour
1 tablespoon sugar
1/3 cup shortening
1 cup buttermilk
1/2 teaspoon baking soda
3/4 pounds sliced bacon, fried and crumbled
1 cup shredded cheddar cheese

Combine flour and sugar. Cut in shortening and set aside. Combine buttermilk and baking soda, stir until baking soda is dissolved. Add buttermilk mixture, bacon and cheese to flour mixture. Stir until dry ingredients are moistened. Turn dough out on lightly floured **No Mess Dough Disc** and knead gently 4 - 5 times. Pat dough to 3/4" thickness and cut with 2" biscuit cutter. Bake at 425° for 10 - 12 minutes. Yield: 12 - 15 biscuits.

Whole Wheat Biscuits

1 cup whole wheat flour
1 cup all - purpose flour
2 teaspoons baking powder
1/2 teaspoon salt
2 tablespoons honey
1/3 cup shortening
1 egg, beaten
3/4 cups skim milk

Sift first four ingredients together. Cut in shortening with pastry blender until mixture resembles coarse meal. Beat milk, egg and honey until well mixed and add to dry ingredients. Mix until moistened. Turn out on lightly floured **No Mess Dough Disc** and knead 4 - 5 times. Pat to 3/4" thickness and cut with biscuit cutter. Bake at 450° for 12 minutes. Yield: 8 - 10 biscuits.

Standard Biscuits

2 cups flour
3 teaspoons baking powder
1/2 teaspoon salt
3 - 4 tablespoons shortening
2/3 - 3/4 cups milk

Sift flour with baking powder and salt; cut in shortening until mixture resembles coarse crumbs. Add milk and mix until dough forms around bowl. Turn out on lightly floured **No Mess Dough Disc**; knead gently 30 seconds. Roll out to 1/2" thickness and cut with biscuit cutter. Bake on ungreased cookie sheet at 450° for 12 - 15 minutes. Yield: 16 biscuits.

Syble's Quick and Easy Biscuits

The secret to these biscuits is to work fast. The faster you get them from the bowl to the oven, the better - this is fast rising dough!

2 cups self rising flour plus 1/4 cup for rolling
1/8 teaspoon baking soda
1 cup buttermilk
grease

Preheat oven to 450° and grease glass pan. Mix flour and baking soda, add buttermilk, stir until smooth. Dough will be soft. Put 1/4 cup flour on **No Mess Dough Disc,** flour top of dough and roll out to 1" in thickness. Cut with biscuit cutter and place in greased pan. Grease tops of biscuits (bacon grease is great!) and bake. Bake at 450° for 12 - 15 minutes or until golden brown.

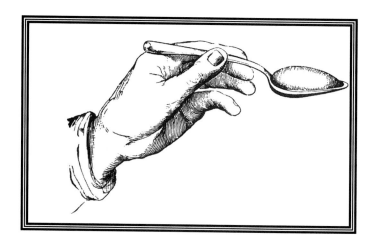

Crunchy Salad Biscuits

1-1/2 cups sifted flour
4 teaspoons baking powder
1 teaspoon salt
1/2 cup uncooked corn grits
1/4 cup shortening
1/4 cup green onions
1/4 cup shredded cheese
1/2 cup milk
1 tablespoon uncooked corn grits

Mix flour, baking powder, salt and 1/2 cup grits in bowl. Add shortening and blend with fork or pastry cutter until crumbly. Stir in green onions and cheese. Slowly add milk and stir to moisten ingredients. Stir to make dough, adding a tablespoon more milk if needed. Turn out on lightly floured **No Mess Dough Disc,** knead gently a few times. Sprinkle disc with 1 tablespoon grits. Roll dough into a 8" x 9" rectangle. Cut into 8 strips 1" wide with the back of a butter knife. Cut each strip into thirds creating 1" x 3" pieces. Place 1" apart on ungreased baking sheet. Bake at 425° for 10 -12 minutes. Yield: 24 biscuits.

Biscuits to Freeze

2 cups all purpose flour
4 teaspoons baking powder
2 teaspoons sugar
1/2 teaspoon salt
1/2 teaspoon cream of tartar
1/2 cup shortening
1 cup milk

Sift dry ingredients. Cut in shortening, add milk and mix with spoon. Turn out on well - floured **No Mess Dough Disc**. Roll to 1" thickness and cut with small biscuit cutter. Freeze on cookie sheet and then store in plastic bags in freezer. Thaw. Bake at 450° for 12 - 15 minutes. Yield: One to two dozen, 2" biscuits.

Freezer Biscuits

5 cups flour
1 teaspoon soda
1 teaspoon salt
4 teaspoons baking powder
4 tablespoons sugar
1 cup shortening
2 packages yeast
1/4 cup warm water
2 cups buttermilk

Dissolve yeast in water. Sift dry ingredients; cut in shortening. Add yeast and milk, mix well. Place on floured **No Mess Dough Disc** and knead quickly. Roll out to 1" thickness and cut with a biscuit cutter. Place on cookie sheet, freeze. After frozen store in plastic bags until ready to bake. To bake, place frozen biscuits in a shallow pan. Place in oven then turn heat to 400°. Biscuits will rise as the oven heats. When oven reaches 400° the baking time will be completed. Total time, about 10 minutes.

Lucky Biscuits

1-3/4 cups unsifted, all purpose flour
3 teaspoons baking powder
3/4 teaspoons salt
1/3 cup shortening
3/4 cups milk

Combine flour, baking powder and salt. Cut in shortening until mixture looks like coarse meal. Add milk, stir with fork until soft dough is formed. Knead lightly on floured **No Mess Dough Disc.** Roll or pat dough to 1/2" in thickness. Cut with floured 2" biscuit cutter. Place on ungreased baking sheet. Bake at 450° 10 -12 minutes. Yield: 16 biscuits

Never Fail Biscuits

1 cup warm water
2 packages yeast
3 tablespoons sugar
3/4 cups oil
2 cups buttermilk
1 teaspoon baking soda
5 cups of self rising flour

Dissolve yeast in water. Add sugar, oil, buttermilk and baking soda. Mix well. Add flour in one cup at a time until mixed. Let rise in a covered bowl for a few hours. Punch down and knead on a lightly floured **No Mess Dough Disc.** Roll out to 3/4" thickness. Cut with floured 2" biscuit cutter. Bake at 450° for 10 - 12 minutes.

Remaining dough can be kept covered and refrigerated for up to one week.

Yeast Bread

2 cups hot water or milk
2 teaspoons salt
1 tablespoon sugar
1 tablespoon shortening or butter
1 cake of yeast
1/2 cup lukewarm water
7 cups flour (plain)

Heat 2 cups water or milk add salt, sugar, shortening or butter. Mix and set aside to cool. Add yeast to lukewarm water, stir to dissolve. Add yeast mixture to above liquid mixture. Sift flour into mixture to make a stiff dough. Turn mixture onto the floured **No Mess Dough Disc** and knead until dough is elastic. Cover and let stand in a warm place until dough is double in bulk. Punch down and turn onto **No Mess Dough Disc,** knead to expel bubbles. Divide dough in two parts and shape into loaves. Place in bread pans. Cover pans and place them in a warm place to rise until three times the original volume. When bread has risen. Bake in pre-heated 375° oven for 30-35 minutes or until golden brown. Brush baked loaves with butter.

Sourdough Bread & Starter

The sourdough starter is the key to this delicious bread. Once you make a batch you can keep it active indefinitely and always have it available for easy baking.

Starter:
1 package yeast
1 cup warm water
2 cups all - purpose flour
3 tablespoons potato flakes
1 cup water
1/2 cup sugar

Combine yeast, water and sugar; stir until yeast is dissolved. Gradually add flour, stirring until smooth. Let stand, loosely covered 24 to 36 hours in a warm place. May be used immediately or stored (loosely covered) in refrigerator. Feed starter at least once a week with: 3 tablespoons potato flakes, 1 cup water and 1/2 cup sugar. Let mixture set overnight and do not use within first three days of feeding.

Bread:
1-1/4 cups sourdough starter
1-1/2 cups water
1/4 cup sugar
1/2 cup cooking oil
2 teaspoons salt
6 cups all purpose flour

Mix ingredients in a large bowl and let set overnight. (Cover with towel or *No Mess Dough Disc* cover). Turn out on lightly floured *No Mess Dough Disc*, knead for 5 - 7 minutes, shape into loaves and put into loaf pans. Let rise again for 6 hours. Bake at 350° for 35 minutes or until golden brown. Yield: 2 - 3 loaves depending on pan size.

Homemade Rolls

1 cup shortening
1 cup sugar
1 teaspoon salt
1 cup boiling water
2 eggs, beaten
2 packages yeast
1 cup warm water
6 cups all purpose flour

In a large bowl mix shortening, sugar, and salt. Pour hot water over mixture. Add eggs and stir together. Dissolve yeast in warm water, add to mixture. Stir in flour. Mix well and refrigerate overnight. Roll out dough on lightly floured **No Mess Dough Disc**. Cut with 2" cutter. Place in greased muffin tins. Let rise until double in size. Bake at 425° for 7 - 8 minutes. Yield: 4 dozen rolls.

Clover Tea Rolls

2 cups all purpose flour, sifted
1/4 cup sugar
3/4 teaspoons baking soda
1/2 teaspoon salt
1/3 cup vegetable shortening
1/2 cup milk
3 tablespoons lemon juice

In a large bowl stir together flour, sugar, baking soda and salt. Cut in shortening until mixture resembles coarse meal. Combine milk and lemon juice; add to flour mixture to make a soft dough. Knead mixture on floured **No Mess Dough Disc**. Form into large marble - sized balls. Place 3 balls into greased muffin tins. Let rise until double in bulk. Bake at 450° for 15 minutes or until light golden brown.

Three - Grain Bread

1 cup water
1/4 cup margarine
13 ounces evaporated milk
1/2 cup honey
1 cup flour
2 cups whole wheat flour
1 cup quick oats
1/2 cup wheat germ
1/2 cup yellow corn meal
2 teaspoons salt
2 packages yeast
2 eggs
3 cups all purpose flour

Heat water, margarine, milk and honey to lukewarm. In a large bowl add 1 cup flour, oats, wheat germ, corn meal, salt and yeast. Beat 2 minutes. Add eggs, beat 2 more minutes, gradually add whole wheat and all purpose flour. Knead until smooth on floured **No Mes**s **Dough Disc** 8 - 10 minutes. Place in bowl, cover and let rise about 1 hour. Divide dough into 2 well - greased loaf pans; cover and let rise until double. Bake at 350° for 50 - 55 minutes.

Homemade Oat Bread

1 cup rolled oats
2 cups boiling water
2 packages yeast in 1/3 cup warm water
1 tablespoon salt
1/2 cup honey
2 tablespoons melted butter
4-1/2 cups flour
poppy seeds

Combine oats and boiling water; let stand 1/2 hour. Combine remaining ingredients, except poppy seeds. Knead on floured **No Mess Dough Disc** for 5-10 minutes until smooth and elastic. Place dough in a large oiled bowl; cover and let rise until double in bulk. Punch down and divide dough in half. Shape into 2 loaves. Grease 2 - 8" x 4" pans, sprinkle with poppy seeds if desired. Let rise to double in bulk. Bake at 325° for 50 minutes.

Quick Vegetable Bread

1 package hot roll mix
1 egg
1-1/2 teaspoons sesame seeds
1/2 teaspoon salt
1/4 cup freshly chopped celery
1/2 cup grated carrots
2 tablespoons green onions, chopped finely
1 pimento, chopped
1/2 cup chopped nuts

Preheat oven to 350° Prepare hot roll mix as directed on package. Add egg and remaining ingredients and mix well. Turn out on lightly floured **No Mess Dough Disc** and knead for 5 minutes. Put in oiled bowl. Lightly brush top of dough with melted butter. Cover and let rise until double in bulk. Punch down and shape into ball. Place in greased 1-1/2 quart pan. Let rise 30 minutes. Brush top with melted butter. Bake 350° for 40 minutes.

Best-Ever Cinnamon Rolls

The fragrance of cinnamon rolls baking in the oven will have your neighbors knocking on your doors, using any excuse for an invitation!

2 packages yeast
2-1/2 cups lukewarm water
1 yellow cake mix
1 cup all purpose flour
3 eggs
1/3 cup of oil
1-1/2 teaspoons salt
5-1/4 cups all purpose flour
soft butter, sugar & cinnamon

Dissolve yeast in warm water for 3 minutes. Add cake mix, 1 cup flour, eggs, oil and salt. Beat well until bubbles appear. Add 5-1/4 cups flour, slowly. Stir until soft dough forms. Knead on well - floured **No Mess Dough Disc** about 5 minutes. Place in greased bowl, let rise in a warm place until double in bulk. Punch down dough, divide into 3 equal parts. Roll out each section of dough on **No Mess Dough Disc,** all the way to the edge of disc. Spread with softened butter, sprinkle with cinnamon and sugar. Roll up like jelly-roll. Cut with dull knife or dental floss into 1" thickness. Place in a greased baking pan and allow to rise until doubled. Bake at 350° for 20 - 30 minutes. Ice with powdered sugar glaze while still hot. Yield: 3 - 4 dozen rolls.

Glaze:

1 pound powdered sugar
1/2 stick melted butter or margarine
1-1/2 teaspoons vanilla
1/2 to 3/4 cups milk

Mix sugar, butter and vanilla. Stir in milk to desired consistency. Drizzle over hot rolls.

Cumin Flatbread

1-1/3 cups warm water
1 envelope dry yeast
3 tablespoons extra virgin olive oil
1 tablespoon minced lemon peel
2-1/4 teaspoons coarse salt
2 teaspoons ground cumin
3 cups bread flour
1 tablespoon cumin seeds
1 tablespoon sesame seeds

Place water in bowl. Sprinkle yeast over water and stir to combine. Let stand 10 minutes. Add oil, lemon peel, salt and ground cumin. Using dough hook or spoon, gradually beat in flour. Continue beating 5 minutes. Turn out dough on floured **No Mess Dough Disc** knead until smooth, about 2 minutes. Lightly oil large bowl, add dough, turn to coat. Cover with plastic wrap, and let rise in warm place until double in size. Preheat oven to 400°. Line 12" x 18" baking sheet with heavy duty foil. Brush foil with oil, press dough in pan using fingertips. Cover pan completely, dough will be thin. Sprinkle with cumin seeds and sesame seeds. Bake at 400° about 30 minutes. Loosen from foil before serving.

Crunchy Caraway Sticks

2 cups flour
3 teaspoons baking powder
1 teaspoon salt
4 tablespoons sugar
1/2 cup shortening
1 tablespoon caraway seeds
3/4 cups milk

Sift together flour, baking powder, salt and sugar. Cut in shortening until mixture is the consistency of corn meal. Add caraway seeds and enough milk to make medium dough. Knead on lightly floured **No Mess Dough Disc** 6 times. Roll out to 1/4" in thickness. Cut into 4" long X 1/4" wide strips. Place on lightly greased baking sheet. Bake at 375° for 10 minutes.

French Bread

2 packages active dry yeast
2-1/2 cups warm water
1 tablespoon salt
2 tablespoons sugar
7 cups bread flour
1 egg white, beaten
cornmeal
butter (to grease pans)

In a large bowl, dissolve yeast in water. Stir in sugar and salt, dissolve. Add 5 cups flour and mix with wooden spoon. Add 1 cup flour and mix until blended. Turn out on floured **No Mess Dough Disc** and knead for 10 minutes, using as much of remaining flour as needed to make dough smooth and elastic. Place dough in greased bowl, turn to coat. Cover with damp cloth and let rise in warm place until double in bulk. Punch down dough and turn out on floured **No Mess Dough Disc** and knead for 2 - 3 minutes. Let dough rest for 15 minutes. Cut dough in 4 pieces and roll each into a rectangle approximately 12" x 15". Roll up dough from long side like a jellyroll. Seal the ends. Grease 4 open ended bread pans with butter. Lightly sprinkle with cornmeal. Place each piece of dough in pan with seam side down. Make four diagonal cuts in each piece of dough. Brush tops with beaten egg white, let dough rise until doubled. Preheat oven to 450°. Spray tops with a fine mist of water and bake 5 minutes. Open oven and spray again. Bake 10 minutes then lower temperature to 350° and bake for 25 minutes. Cool on wire rack. Yield: 4 Baguettes. Note: Bread may be wrapped in foil and frozen, then re-heated at 350°.

Crusty Dill Bread

1 package dry yeast
2 cups warm water
3/4 cup cottage cheese
1/2 cup sugar
1/4 cup margarine or butter
1 tablespoon dill seed
2 teaspoons salt
6-1/2 - 7 cups flour
butter or margarine, melted for crust

Dissolve yeast in water. Heat cheese, then cool to warm and add to yeast mixture with sugar, butter, dill seed and salt. Add half the flour and mix well. Add enough of remaining flour to make a soft dough that leaves the sides of bowl. Knead on floured **No Mess Dough Disc** until smooth. Put dough in greased bowl, turn to coat. Cover and let rise in warm place until double in bulk. Punch down, divide dough and shape into two loaves. Place in greased baking pans. Let rise in warm place until double in bulk. Bake at 350° for 45 - 60 minutes. Remove from pans, cool. Brush with melted butter or margarine and sprinkle with salt.

Homemade Crackers

2 cups flour
1/2 teaspoon salt
1 tablespoon sugar
1/8 cup margarine
1/2 cup milk

Mix ingredients together to form dough. Roll out on lightly floured **No Mess Dough Disc** to paper thin consistency. Sprinkle with sesame or poppy seeds for variation. Cut into small squares or rounds and prick surface of dough with fork. Bake at 400° for 10 - 12 minutes.

Cheese Bread

1 package dry yeast
3/4 cups warm water
2-1/2 to 3 cups flour
1/4 cup instant dry non - fat milk
or 1 tablespoon regular dry non - fat milk
1 tablespoon sugar
1 teaspoon salt
1 egg
1 cup finely shredded cheese

Dissolve yeast in water. Mix 2-1/2 cups of flour with remaining dry ingredients. Add dissolved yeast, egg, and cheese, adding more flour if needed to make dough easy to handle. Knead dough on lightly floured **No Mess Dough Disc** about 10 minutes. Place in greased bowl, turn to coat. Cover lightly and let rise in warm place until double in bulk. Punch down, cover and let rise 30 minutes until almost double. Shape into one round loaf. Place on greased baking sheet or pan. Cover with greased wax paper and let rise 1 hour. Bake at 375° for 30 - 35 minutes.

Party Bread Sticks

3 - 3-1/2 cups flour
1 tablespoon sugar
1 teaspoon salt
2 packages active dry yeast
1/4 cup olive oil or salad oil
1-1/4 cups hot water
1 egg white, beaten with 1 tablespoon water
coarse salt, toasted sesame seeds, or poppy seeds

In the large bowl of an electric mixer, add 1 cup of flour, sugar, salt and yeast, stirring to blend. Add oil, then gradually stir in hot water and beat on medium speed for 2 minutes. Add 1/2 cup flour and beat on high speed for 2 minutes. Add remaining flour to make a soft dough. Turn dough out on well-floured **No Mess Dough Disc** and shape dough into a smooth ball, log or block. Use the back of a butter knife and cut into 20 equal pieces. Roll each piece into a rope 16" long. Arrange 1" apart on oiled baking sheets. Brush with egg wash mixture. Sprinkle with your choice of salt or seeds. Bake at 375° for 10 - 15 minutes.

Homemade Bread

1 package yeast
1 cup warm water
1/4 cup dry milk
1/4 cup sugar
1/4 cup oil
1 egg
2 teaspoons salt
3-1/2 to 4 cups flour

Put water in large bowl and dissolve yeast. Add milk, sugar, oil, egg, salt and 1-1/2 cups flour. Beat 3 minutes with electric mixer. Add remaining flour and mix well. Turn out on floured **No Mess Dough Disc** and knead for 3 minutes until dough is elastic and smooth. Roll out dough on **No Mess Dough Disc**. Start at one end and roll dough up tightly. Place in greased 9" x 5" x 3" bread pan, seam side down. Let rise 1 hour. Bake at 375° for 35 minutes.

Easy Anadama Bread

5-1/2 - 6-1/2 cups flour
2-1/2 teaspoons salt
1 cup yellow corn meal
2 packages active dry yeast
1/4 cup butter or margarine, softened
2 cups hot water
1/2 cup molasses

Mix 2-1/2 cups of flour, salt, corn meal, and yeast together. Add butter and gradually stir in water and molasses. Beat 2 minutes on medium speed or 300 strokes by hand. Add 1/2 cup more flour to thicken batter, beat 2 minutes longer. Stir in enough flour to make a soft dough. Knead dough on lightly floured **No Mess Dough Disc** until smooth and elastic, about 5 - 10 minutes. Place dough in greased bowl, turn to coat. Cover and let rise in a warm place until double in bulk. Punch down in bowl. Turn out on lightly floured **No Mess Dough Disc**. Shape into 2 loaves. Put in greased baking pans. Cover and let rise until double in size. Bake at 375° about 35 minutes. Remove from pans and cool on racks.

Parmesan Break Aparts

1/3 cup butter
2-1/4 cups flour
1 tablespoon sugar (optional)
2-1/2 teaspoons baking powder
1 teaspoon salt
1 clove garlic, minced
1 cup milk
2 - 3 tablespoons butter, melted
1 - 2 cups freshly grated Parmesan cheese
1 tablespoon finely chopped parsley
1/2 teaspoon garlic salt
dash paprika

Preheat oven to 450°. Melt butter in 9" x 13" baking dish. Sift flour, sugar, baking powder and salt into large mixing bowl. Add minced garlic to flour mixture. Add milk and mix with fork or pastry blender until mixture clings together. Knead dough slightly on lightly floured **No Mess Dough Disc** then roll to 3/4" thickness and cut into 3" to 6" long strips, 1" wide. Place in the buttered dish and brush with melted butter. Sprinkle with Parmesan cheese, parsley, garlic salt and paprika. Bake at 450° for 15 minutes or until golden brown. Serve hot.

Variation:

Add 1/2 cup cheddar cheese to mixture and omit toppings.

Notes:_____

_____
_____
_____
_____
_____
_____
_____
_____
_____
_____
_____
_____
_____
_____
_____
_____
_____
_____
_____

Braided Italian Bread

3 cups warm water
2 packages yeast
4 tablespoons sugar
10 cups unbleached white flour
4 teaspoons salt
4 eggs
3 tablespoons oil
1 egg for glaze

Mix water, yeast, and sugar. Let it sit until all ingredients are dissolved. With a wooden spoon, mix flour, salt, eggs and oil with yeast mixture. Mix well and turn out on floured **No Mess Dough Disc.** Knead mixture until smooth and elastic. Place dough in lightly greased bowl, turn to coat and let rise in a warm place until double in bulk. Punch down and divide dough into 3 parts. Divide each part into 3 sections. Roll each section into a 12" rope. Braid each group of 3, pinching the ends to seal. On a lightly greased baking sheet, let rise until double in size. Brush with slightly beaten egg. Bake at 375° for 30 minutes or until golden brown. Yield: 3 loaves.

Cream Cheese Crescents

1-1/8 cups butter
8 ounce package cream cheese, whipped
2-1/2 cups flour
1/4 teaspoon salt
confectioners sugar
preserves or cinnamon sugar/ nut mixture

Blend butter, cheese, flour and salt. Chill well. Roll dough 1/4" thick on floured **No Mess Dough Disc** dusted with confectioners sugar. Cut into small triangles, about 4". Spread with preserves or top with cinnamon sugar/ nut mixture. Roll up from wide end to the point. Bend ends to form crescents. Bake 375° oven for 20 minutes.

Doughnuts

Homemade doughnuts are so fresh, fast and delicious that you'll be tempted to set up your own coffee shop.

4 eggs, beaten
1 cup sugar
1/3 cup buttermilk
1/3 cup shortening, melted
3-1/2 cups flour
2 teaspoons baking powder
3/4 teaspoons salt
1/2 teaspoon nutmeg

Beat eggs and sugar until light, add buttermilk and cooled shortening. Add dry ingredients. Mix until smooth, chill dough. Roll out on **No Mess Dough Disc** to 3/8" thick. Cut with doughnut cutter. Let stand 15 minutes. Fry in hot oil until golden brown. Yield: Two dozen.

Chocolate Doughnuts

1 package dry yeast
1/4 cup warm water
1 cup milk
3/4 cups sugar
2/3 cups cocoa
1/3 cup butter
1-1/2 teaspoons salt
3 eggs, beaten
1-1/2 teaspoons vanilla
5 cups flour
confectioners sugar

Soften yeast in warm water. Heat milk, sugar, cocoa, butter and salt. Stir until butter is melted. Cool to lukewarm. Beat eggs in large bowl, add vanilla, yeast and milk mixture. Slowly stir in flour, 1 cup at a time until well blended. Chill dough. Roll out on **No Mess Dough Disc** to 1/2" thick. Cut with doughnut cutter. Place on lightly greased cookie sheet and cover to let rise until dough is double in bulk, about 1-1/2 hours. Fry in hot oil for 2-1/2 - 3 minutes. Drain and roll in confectioners sugar.

Jelly Filled Doughnuts

1 package hot roll mix
3/4 cups sugar
3/4 cups very warm water
1 jar strawberry preserves
vegetable oil for frying

Prepare hot roll mix with 3 tablespoons of sugar and water. Let rise following label instructions. Turn dough out on lightly floured **No Mess Dough Disc.** Knead 8 - 10 times, then roll out to 1/2" in thickness. Cut with floured 2-1/2" cutter. Place on lightly greased cookie sheet. Roll again and cut left over dough. Cover with clean towel, let rise until double in bulk. Fill a large saucepan or skillet 2/3 full of vegetable oil and heat to 370° (use a deep -fat thermometer). Fry 2 - 3 doughnuts at a time, turning once until golden brown. Drop hot doughnuts into bowl with remaining sugar, coat evenly and cool. Cut a slit in side of doughnut. Fill pastry bag with preserves, place tip in doughnut opening and fill. Use a cake decorator if you don't have a pastry bag.

Yeast Doughnuts

2 cups lukewarm milk
2 packages yeast
1/2 cup sugar
1 teaspoon salt
1/2 cup shortening
2 eggs, beaten
7 cups flour

Dissolve yeast in milk. Add sugar and salt to yeast, stir. In large bowl mix shortening and eggs. Add liquid ingredients mix until well blended. Slowly add flour and knead into soft dough. Let rise until double in bulk, then place on floured **No Mess Dough Disc**. Roll to 1/2", thick and cut with doughnut cutter. Let rise again for 30 minutes and fry in 1" hot oil until golden brown. Glaze or sugar if desired.

Doughnut Glaze:

2 cups sugar
1/2 cup butter
3/4 cups milk
1 teaspoon vanilla

Cook to soft ball stage when dropped in cold water. Dip or drip onto warm doughnuts.

Old - Fashioned Doughnuts

3 tablespoons shortening, melted
1 cup milk
3/4 cups sugar
1 teaspoon salt
1 egg, beaten
1 teaspoon nutmeg
1 package yeast
1/2 cup warm water
4 cups flour
2 cups powdered sugar
1/2 cup evaporated milk

Mix shortening, milk, sugar and salt. Add egg and nutmeg. Stir yeast into 1/2 cup warm water, dissolve. Add enough flour to make dough. Knead on floured **No Mess Dough Disc**; roll out to 1/2" in thickness and cut. Place on floured baking sheet and let rise until double in bulk. Deep fry in hot oil; drain on paper towels. Mix powdered sugar, evaporated milk and a little water. Dip hot doughnuts in sugar mixture to glaze.

Notes:_____

_____

_____

_____

_____

_____

_____

_____

_____

_____

_____

_____

_____

_____

_____

_____

_____

_____

_____

_____

_____

_____

COOKIES

Left to right: Great Gingerbread, Two - Toned Rolled Cookies, Snowflake Cookies, Sugar Cookies and Stoplight Cookies.

Honey Lemon Cookies

1/3 cup sugar
1/3 cup shortening
2/3 cups honey
1 egg
1 teaspoon lemon extract
2-3/4 cups flour
1 teaspoon baking soda
1 teaspoon salt

Heat oven to 375°. Mix sugar, shortening, honey, egg and lemon extract. Stir in remaining ingredients. Roll to 1/4" thickness on lightly floured **No Mess Dough Disc**. Cut to desired shapes with cookie cutters. Place 1" apart on lightly greased cookie sheet. Bake until no indentations remain when touched, approximately 7 - 8 minutes. Cool. Yield: 2-1/2 dozen.

Jam Sandwich Cookies

2 cups flour
3/4 cups butter, softened
1/3 cup sugar
1/2 teaspoon salt
2 eggs
1/3 cup jam (any flavor)
vanilla Frosting

Heat oven to 375°. Mix flour, butter, sugar, salt and eggs. Roll to 1/8" thickness on lightly floured **No Mess Dough Disc**. Cut into 2" rounds. Place on ungreased cookie sheet. Bake until set, 8 - 10 minutes. Remove and cool. Spread jam on cookie and sandwich with top cookie. Frost with vanilla frosting.

Vanilla Frosting
1 cup powdered sugar
1 tablespoon butter, softened,
1 tablespoon plus 1 teaspoon milk
1/4 teaspoon vanilla

Beat until smooth, adding milk to desired consistency.

Applesauce Cookies

1 cup butter or margarine
1 teaspoon baking soda
3 cups flour
2 cups sugar
4 tablespoons applesauce
2 eggs
2 teaspoons baking powder
1 teaspoon vanilla

Mix butter and sugar until creamy; add eggs, applesauce, baking soda and vanilla. Sift flour, baking powder and add to mixture.(Add enough flour to make a soft dough.) Roll out on **No Mess Dough Disc** to 1/4" thickness and cut to desired shapes. Bake at 375° for 8 - 10 minutes.

Great Gingerbread Cookies

1/2 cup butter or margarine
1/2 cup brown sugar
1/2 cup molasses
1 egg
3-1/2 cups all - purpose flour
1 teaspoon baking powder
1/2 teaspoon baking soda
1/2 teaspoon salt
1 teaspoon cinnamon
1 teaspoon ginger
1/4 teaspoon nutmeg
1/4 teaspoon ground cloves
1/2 cup buttermilk

Mix butter and sugar until light and fluffy. Add molasses and egg, mixing thoroughly. Add flour, baking soda, baking powder, spices and salt; mix well. Add buttermilk and mix. Shape dough into a ball, cover and chill for 2 hours. Place dough on lightly floured **No Mess Dough Disc** and roll to 1/4" thickness. Cut into desired shapes. Bake 8 - 10 minutes at 375°. Yield: 3 dozen.

HINTS FOR COOKIES

If dough is too soft, add 1 or 2 tablespoons of flour.

If dough is too dry, add 1 or 2 tablespoons of milk or cream.

When mixing cookie dough, always mix thoroughly.

Always use butter or shortening at room temperature and never substitute oil.

Step - by - Step Cookies

Chill dough for best results.

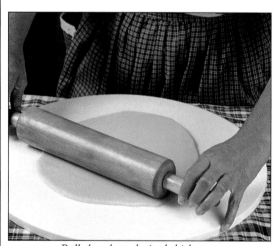

Roll dough to desired thickness.

Use floured cookie cutters and cut to shape.

<u>Cookie Notes:</u>

Turnover Surprise

1 cup sugar
1/2 cup shortening
2 eggs
1 teaspoon vanilla
2-1/2 cups flour
1/2 teaspoon salt
1/4 teaspoon baking soda
cherry or pineapple filling
milk
sugar

Mix 1 cup sugar, shortening, eggs and vanilla. Stir in flour, salt and baking soda. Cover and refrigerate for 1 hour. Prepare filling. Heat oven to 400°. Roll dough out on lightly floured **No Mess Dough Disc.** Cut into 3" rounds or squares. Spoon about 1 teaspoon filling into half of each circle. Fold dough over filling; pinch edges to seal. Place 1" apart on ungreased cookie sheet. Brush with milk; sprinkle with sugar. Bake until very light brown, 8 - 10 minutes. Remove immediately from cookie sheet and cool. Yield: 4-1/2 dozen.

Cherry Filling:

3/4 cups sugar
3/4 cups orange juice
18 maraschino cherries
3 tablespoons cornstarch
1/2 cup maraschino cherry syrup
1 tablespoon plus 1-1/2 teaspoon butter

Mix sugar and cornstarch in saucepan. Stir in orange juice gradually. Stir in remaining ingredients. Cook stirring constantly until mixture thickens and boils. Cool completely before using.

Pineapple Filling:

1 (13 - 1/4 ounce) can crushed pineapple
2/3 cup sugar
3 tablespoons flour
2 tablespoons lemon juice
1 tablespoon butter
Dash of ground nutmeg

Drain pineapple, reserving 1/2 cup syrup. Mix sugar and flour in saucepan. Stir in pineapple, syrup and remaining ingredients. Cook, stirring constantly until mixture thickens. Cool completely before using.

Coconut Cookies

1/2 cup shortening
1 egg, well beaten
1 cup light brown sugar
1/4 teaspoon salt
2 cups flour
1/4 teaspoon baking powder
1 cup shredded coconut
1 teaspoon vanilla extract

Cream shortening, beat in sugar, vanilla and egg. Mix dry ingredients together in separate bowl. Add dry ingredients to creamed mixture. Mix together thoroughly. Roll out 1/8" thick on **No Mess Dough Disc**. Cut into desired shapes with floured cookie cutter. Bake at 375° for 8 - 10 minutes.

Linda's Sugar Cookies

1/2 cup shortening
1/4 cup butter
1 cup sugar
2 eggs
1/2 teaspoon lemon or vanilla flavoring
2-1/2 cups all purpose flour
1 teaspoon baking powder
1 teaspoon salt

Mix together shortening, butter, sugar, eggs and flavoring. Sift flour, baking powder and salt in separate bowl. Mix dry ingredients into creamed mixture. Chill at least 1 hour. Preheat oven to 350.° Roll out dough on lightly floured **No Mess Dough Disc** and cut to desired shapes. Bake until light brown on bottom, about 6 - 10 minutes.

Ginger Snaps

1 cup molasses
1/2 cup sugar
1/2 cup butter, softened
2-1/2 cups flour
1 teaspoon ginger
1/4 teaspoon salt

Stir molasses, sugar and butter together. Mix in flour, ginger and salt. Roll out on **No Mess Dough Disc** as thin as possible. Cut to desired shape. Bake at 325° until golden brown.

Almond Tea Cookies

14 ounces butter
1/2 cup sugar
1 teaspoon almond or vanilla extract
3/4 pound of ground almonds
3 cups flour
pinch of salt

Cream butter, sugar and extract together. Add almonds and work in flour and salt. Place on floured **No Mess Dough Disc** and roll to 1/2" thickness. Cut in finger lengths, 1" x 3". Bake in moderate oven, 350° about 20 minutes. Roll in powdered sugar while slightly warm.

Shortbread Cookies

1/2 cup powdered sugar, packed
1 cup butter
3/4 teaspoon salt
1 teaspoon vanilla
2 cups flour
2 tablespoons milk

Cream all ingredients except flour. Lightly stir in flour to make a soft dough. Put on lightly floured **No Mess Dough Disc.** Roll out to 1/3" thickness. Cut into rectangles 1" x 2". Place on ungreased cookie sheet. Prick each cookie 2 - 3 times with a fork. Bake at 350° for 12-20 minutes until lightly browned. Yield: 2 dozen cookies.

Chocolate Cookies

1 cup light brown sugar
1/2 cup butter
1 tablespoon cream
1/2 cup milk
1-1/2 cups flour
1/2 cup cocoa
1 egg, well - beaten
1 teaspoon vanilla extract
3/4 cups chopped nuts
1-1/2 teaspoon baking powder
1/3 teaspoon salt

Cream butter. Mix in sugar and egg. Add cream, milk and vanilla extract. Mix dry ingredients together in separate bowl, then add to creamed mixture. Add nuts and mix well. Roll out on floured **No Mess Dough Disc**. Cut into desired shapes with floured cookie cutters and place on ungreased cookie sheet. Sprinkle with sugar. Bake at 400° for 10 minutes.

Jam - Filled Cocoa Cookies

3/4 cup butter or margarine, softened
1 can sweetened condensed milk
2 eggs
2 teaspoons vanilla
2 - 3/4 cups all purpose flour
2/3 cup cocoa
2 teapoons baking powder
1/2 teaspoon baking soda
1/2 cup ground almonds
preserves or jam
powdered sugar

In a large bowl mix butter, milk, eggs and vanillla until well blended. Stir together dry ingredients; gradually add to butter mixture, beating until well blended. Stir in almonds. Divide dough into fourths; wrap each in plastic wrap. Refrigerate at least 3 hours. Heat oven to 350°. Roll one portion at a time on lightly floured **No Mess Dough Disc** (keep remaining dough chilled). Roll out to 1/8" thickness. Cut into an equal number of 2" rounds. Place half the rounds on greased cookie sheet. Spread about 1/4 teaspoon preserves in center of each round. Using 1" round or small star shaped cutter, cut shape from center of remaining rounds. Place cut out rounds on filled rounds and press edges together to seal. Bake 6 minutes or until set. Cool, sprinkle with powdered sugar if desired. Yield: 5 - 1/2 dozen cookies.

Variation

To make plain cocoa cookies, roll out dough and cut with cookie cutter. Place on greased cookie sheet and bake at 350° until set, about 5 minutes.

<u>Brown Sugar Cookies</u>

2 cups flour
1-1/2 teaspoon baking powder
1/3 teaspoon salt
1/2 cup butter
1/2 cup brown sugar, packed
1 egg
1 tablespoon cream or half & half
1-1/2 teaspoon vanilla extract

Blend 1 cup flour, baking powder and salt. In separate bowl cream butter, sugar, beaten egg, vanilla extract and cream. Stir flour into creamed mixture adding flour as needed to make a stiff dough. Wrap in wax paper, chill for several hours. Place on lightly floured **No Mess Dough Disc** and roll out to 1/8" thickness. Use floured cutters and place on ungreased baking sheet, sprinkle with sugar. Bake at 375°, 8 - 10 minutes.

<u>Sour Cream Cookies</u>

1 cup sugar
1/4 cup margarine or butter, softened
1/4 cup shortening
1 egg
1 teaspoon vanilla
2 2/3 cups all purpose flour
1 teaspoon baking powder
1/2 teaspoon baking soda
1/2 teaspoon salt
1/4 teaspoon ground nutmeg
1/2 cup dairy sour cream
Decorators' Frosting (below)

Heat oven to 425°. Mix 1 cup sugar, the margarine, shortening, egg and vanilla. Stir in remaining ingredients. Divide dough into 3 equal parts. Roll each part to 1/4" thickness on lightly floured **No Mess Dough Disk**. Cut into desired shapes with 2" cookie cutter. Place about 1 inch apart on ungreased cookie sheet. Bake until no indentation remains when touched, 6 to 8 minutes. 4 to 5 Dozen. If using self-rising flour, omit baking powder, baking soda and salt.

Variations:

Chocolate Sour Cream Cookies: Mix 1 ounce melted unsweetened chocolate (cool) into 1 part dough.

Coconut Sour Cream Cookies: Mix 1/4 cup cookie coconut into 1 part dough.

Orange Sour Cream Cookies: Mix 1 tablespoon grated orange peel into 1 part dough.

Peanut Butter Sour Cream Cookies: Mix 1 tablespoon creamy peanut butter into 1 part dough.

Soft Molasses Cookies

4-1/2 cups flour
1 teaspoon soda
2 teaspoons baking powder
3 teaspoons ginger
1/2 teaspoon salt
1 cup butter, softened
1 cup light brown sugar, packed
2 eggs
3/4 cups molasses
3/4 cups sour milk*
2 teaspoons vanilla extract

Mix butter and sugar together. Add beaten eggs, molasses and vanilla. Add dry ingredients to creamed mixture alternating with milk; beat after each addition. Chill 2 - 3 hours. Roll out 1/8" thick on lightly floured *No Mess Dough Disc.* Cut and sprinkle with sugar. Bake at 375° for 12 minutes.

*To make sour milk, add 1 tablespoon vinegar or lemon juice.

Date - Filled Oatmeal Cookies

1 cup butter, softened
1 cup brown sugar, packed
1/2 teaspoon soda dissolved in
1/2 cup hot water
2 cups uncooked oatmeal
2 cups flour
2 teaspoons baking powder
1 teaspoon vanilla extract

Blend all ingredients. Chill dough. Prepare filling. Roll out dough on lightly floured *No Mess Dough Disc*, as thin as possible. Cut dough into desired shapes. Add 1 teaspoon filling and cover with second piece of dough; seal edges. Bake at 350° until golden.

Date Filling

1 package dates, pitted and chopped
1 cup sugar
1 cup cold water
1/2 teaspoon vanilla

Cook mixture until thick. Cool and spread on cookies. Cover with dough and bake as directed.

Coconut Washboards

3/4 cups butter, softened
1 cup packed brown sugar
1 egg
1 teaspoon vanilla extract
1/2 teaspoon almond extract
2 cups flour
3/4 teaspoons baking powder
1/8 teaspoon salt
1/4 teaspoon cinnamon
1/4 teaspoon nutmeg
1-3/4 cups coconut

Mix butter and sugar until creamy. Add egg, vanilla and almond extract. Combine flour, baking powder, salt and spices. Stir into butter mixture. Add coconut, mix well. Chill dough about 1-1/2 hours. Shape into eight 16" long rolls. Use slightly floured **No Mess Dough Disc**. Flatten dough to 1" in width (do not stretch lengthwise.) Cut into 2" sections and place on ungreased baking sheet. Press ridges on top of cookies with a fork. Bake at 375° for 8 -10 minutes. Yield: 6-1/2 dozen cookies.

*Note: Cookies can be rolled out on **No Mess Dough Disc** and cut with floured cookie cutters.*

Two - Toned Rolled Cookies

2 cups flour
1 teaspoon baking powder
1/4 teaspoon salt
1/2 cup butter, softened
1 cup sugar
1 egg
1 teaspoon vanilla extract
1/4 teaspoon almond extract
3/4 cups coconut
1/2 package sweet chocolate, melted and slightly cooled

Mix flour, baking powder and salt together. In separate bowl cream butter; add sugar. Beat in egg, vanilla and almond extract. Add flour mixture to creamed mixture a little at a time until smooth. Divide dough in half. Stir coconut into half of dough; add chocolate to remaining half. Chill about 1 hour. Roll out to 1/8" in thickness on floured **No Mess Dough Disc.** Cut in desired shapes with floured cookie cutters. Place on ungreased baking sheets. Bake at 400° for 5 - 8 minutes. Cool and store in airtight containers. Yield: 5 dozen cookies.

Pinwheel Cookies

Roll out chocolate and vanilla sections and layer one on top of the other. Roll up jellyroll style and cut into 1/4" slices.

Butter Cookies

1 cup butter
1 cup sugar
1/2 teaspoon vanilla extract
1/2 teaspoon lemon extract
2 eggs, beaten
2-1/4 cups flour
1 teaspoon cream of tartar
1/2 teaspoon baking soda

Cream butter, sugar and extracts together. Add beaten eggs. In separate bowl mix dry ingredients together and then mix into creamed mixture. Chill dough. Roll out thinly on lightly floured **No Mess Dough Disc**. Cut and sprinkle with sugar. Decorate with bits of candied cherry. Bake at 375° for 8 - 10 minutes.

Cinnamon Tarts

1 cup butter
2 cups sugar
2 eggs
1 egg, separated
2 teaspoons vanilla
4 cups all purpose flour
cinnamon and sugar, mixed

Cream sugar and butter together thoroughly. Add eggs and egg yolk; beat well. Add vanilla; and mix in flour; blend well. Roll dough on floured **No Mess Dough Disc** to 1/4" thickness. Cut into desired shapes. Beat egg white and brush over cookies. Sprinkle with cinnamon and sugar mixture. Place on greased cookie sheet 2 inches apart. Bake at 350° for 8 to 10 minutes.

Old - Fashioned Sugar Cookies

The classic sugar cookie is so fast and easy with the No Mess Dough Disc. Make a double batch of dough and keep it frozen for an emergency.

1/2 cup butter (1 stick)
3/4 cups sugar
1 egg
1/2 teaspoon vanilla
1/2 teaspoon lemon rind
2 cups flour
1/2 teaspoon baking powder
1/2 teaspoon salt
2 tablespoons milk

Thoroughly cream butter, sugar, and egg together. Add vanilla and lemon rind. Sift dry ingredients together and add alternately with milk. Mix thoroughly. Roll out to 1/8" thickness on floured **No Mess Dough Disc**. Sprinkle with sugar and cut with cookie cutter. Bake at 375° for 10 - 12 minutes.

Lemon Wafers

1 cup butter
2 cups sugar
3 eggs, well - beaten
3 tablespoons lemon juice
2 teaspoons baking powder
4 cups flour
1 teaspoon lemon extract
1 egg white, beaten

Mix butter, sugar, eggs, lemon juice and lemon extract. Add flour and baking powder. Chill dough. Roll out thinly on floured **No Mess Dough Disc.** Cut into desired shapes with floured cookie cutters. Brush with egg whites and sprinkle with sugar before baking. Bake at 375° for 8 - 10 minutes.

Snowflake Cookies

1 cup sugar
3/4 cup butter, softened
2 eggs
1 teaspoon vanilla or 1/2 teaspoon lemon extract
2-1/2 cups flour
1 teaspoon baking powder
1 teaspoon salt
1 container (16.5 oz.) vanilla ready to spread frosting

Mix sugar, butter, eggs and flavoring extract. Stir in flour, baking powder and salt. Cover and refrigerate at least 1 hour. Heat oven to 400°. Roll dough 1/8" thickness on lightly floured **No Mess Dough Disc.** Cut into 2-1/2" star shapes. Place on ungreased cookie sheet; bake for 8 - 10 minutes; cool. Put cookies together in stacked pairs (do not match points on stars) with 1/4 teaspoon frosting . Heat remaining frosting over low heat until thin. Tint with food color if desired. Pour about 1 teaspoon frosting over each pair of stars. Yield: 2 dozen cookies.

Paintbrush Cookies

Prepare dough as directed for Snowflake Cookies. After rolling out dough on **No Mess Dough Disc** cut into desired shapes with cookie cutters. Paint designs on cookies with egg yolk paint, use small brushes. Bake as directed.

Egg Yolk Paint

Mix egg yolk and 1/4 teaspoon water. Divide mixture among several small custard cups. Tint each with different food color to make bright colors. If paint thickens, stir in a few drops of water.

Stoplight Cookies

Prepare dough as directed for Snowflake Cookies. After rolling dough on **No Mess Dough Disc** cut into 2" x 3" rectangles. Make three depressions with the end of a wooden spoon to represent the stoplight and fill with red, yellow and green jams or jellies of your choice. "We use raspberry, mint and apricot". Bake as directed.

Christmas Cookies

1 cup butter, softened
1 cup sugar
2 eggs
1/2 cup blanched almonds, ground
1 teaspoon vanilla, lemon or almond extract
2-1/2 cups flour
1/2 teaspoon salt
1 teaspoon cinnamon
2 teaspoons baking powder
1 egg white, beaten

Mix softened butter and sugar together. Beat eggs well and add to creamed mixture. Add nuts and flavoring extract. Mix flour, salt, cinnamon and baking powder in a separate bowl and then add to creamed mixture. Roll out on floured **No Mess Dough Disc.** Cut into fancy shapes. Brush each top with egg white. Place on greased cookie sheet. Bake at 375° for 10 minutes.

Old Fashioned Molasses Cookies

1/2 cup butter, softened
3/4 cup sugar
1 egg
1 cup molasses
1 teaspoon vanilla
2 3/4 - 3 cups flour
1/2 teaspoon baking soda
2 teaspoons baking powder
1 teaspoon cinnamon
2 teaspoons ginger
1/2 teaspoon nutmeg
1/2 teaspoon salt
1 cup sour milk (see p. 64)

Cream butter; add sugar, egg, molasses, and vanilla. In a separate bowl mix together dry ingredients. Add sour milk to butter mixture. Add flour mixture to creamed ingredients, mix thoroughly and chill. Roll out dough to 1/8" thickness on lightly floured **No Mess Dough Disc.** Cut to desired shapes. Bake at 375° for 12 minutes.

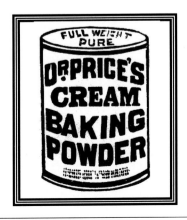

Tea Cookies

2-1/2 cups flour
1 cup butter
1 cup sugar
1/2 teaspoon salt
2 eggs
2 teaspoons vanilla

Mix butter, sugar and salt. Stir in eggs and vanilla. Slowly stir in flour, mix well. Wrap in wax paper and chill for 4 - 5 hours. Divide into thirds and roll out 3/16" thick on floured **No Mess Dough Disc.** Cut with 2" cookie cutters. Place on ungreased baking sheet. Bake at 375° for 8 - 10 minutes. Yield: 11 - 12 dozen cookies.

Spicy Delights

1 cup shortening
1 cup sugar
2 cups molasses
8 ounces sour cream
1-1/2 teaspoons baking soda
dash of salt
1-1/2 teaspoons cinnamon
1-1/2 teaspoons ground allspice
1-1/2 teaspoons ground cloves
1 cup chopped pecans
7 cups all purpose flour

Put shortening in large bowl and slowly add sugar; beat until light and fluffy. Add molasses, sour cream, baking soda, salt and spices; beat well and add pecans. Mix in flour to form a stiff dough. Divide dough into 4 parts; cover and chill overnight. Roll out 1 section at a time on lightly floured **No Mess Dough Disc**. Keep remaining dough chilled until ready to use. Cut into desired shapes with cookie cutters and place 2" apart on greased cookie sheet. Bake at 350° for 10 - 12 minutes. Yield: 15 dozen medium cookies.

Top left, clockwise: Swedish Tea Ring, Sopapillas, Chili Shrimp Quiche, Empanadas, Pot Stickers and Pasta.

Flour Tortillas

Flour tortillas are a staple for many south of the border countries. Making tortillas at home gives you the option to make them as big or small as needed. They're so versatile you can eat them from morning until night.

1 pound all purpose or whole wheat flour
1 tablespoon salt
6 tablespoons lard or shortening
1 cup of hot water

Sift the flour and salt into a bowl; and cut in lard until it resembles corn meal. Gradually mix in water to form a soft dough. Knead on floured **No Mess Dough Disc** until smooth and no longer sticky. Cover with a damp tea towel. Cut off about 3 tablespoons of dough at a time (keeping the rest covered.) Knead into a ball. Roll dough out onto lightly floured **No Mess Dough Disc** into a very thin circle. Cut out using a 10" plate as a guide. Stack the tortillas as you make them flouring well to prevent sticking or adding a sheet of wax paper between each layer. Cook as needed in hot skillet about 10 seconds per side. Keep stack covered until all are cooked.

Spanish Flour Tortillas

3 cups flour
2 teaspoons salt
5 tablespoons lard or shortening
3/4 cups hot water

Mix flour and salt; cut in shortening and add hot water. Knead on lightly floured **No Mess Dough Disc**. Pinch off 1" pieces and knead into patties. Roll out to 1/8" in thickness. Cook on hot, ungreased griddle until spotted with brown color. Stack together and wrap in towel while cooking, tortillas will stay warm for 30 minutes. As the tortillas cool, they will become brittle, but can be re-heated on a hot griddle to soften.

Sopapillas

Sopapillas, or "little pillows," are a favorite accompaniment to many Mexican dishes. The traditional method of serving is with a generous portion of sweet, honey which contrasts the spiciness of the dish.

4 cups of flour
3/4 teaspoons salt
3 teaspoons baking powder
1-1/2 tablespoons shortening
1-1/4 cups water
2 - 3 tablespoons sugar (optional)

Mix all ingredients and knead until smooth on a lightly floured **No Mess Dough Disc.** Cover and let stand one half hour. Roll to 1/8" thickness on **No Mess Dough Disc**. Cut into 3" squares. Fry in hot, deep fat.

Empanadas

Empanadas are served from Mexico to the tip of South America and have a variety of fillings from sweet to savory. The version featured here is Mexican and makes a wonderful luncheon entree, hors d'oeuvre or snack.

Use pastry from Chili Shrimp Quiche (page 77)

Filling:

1 onion, chopped
1 clove garlic, finely chopped
1 small green pepper, seeded and chopped
1 tablespoon oil
8 ounces ground beef
1 tablespoon flour
1/2 teaspoon ground cumin
1/2 teaspoon paprika
1/2 teaspoon dried oregano, crushed
salt & pepper
1 - 2 chilies, seeded and chopped
2 tablespoons tomato paste
3 tablespoons water
2 tablespoons sliced almonds

Prepare the pastry. Cook the onions, garlic and green pepper in oil until soft. Add the meat and fry until browned. Add flour, spices, oregano and seasonings. Stir well and cook briefly before adding chilies, tomato paste and water. Cook slowly for 10 - 15 minutes. Add almonds and allow to cool. Roll out the pastry on floured **No Mess Dough Disc** and cut into 6" rounds using a 6" plate as a guide. Place the cooled filling on one side of the pastry round and dampen the edges with water. Fold over and press to seal edges. Crimp the edges with a fork. Place on baking sheet. Prick the pastry surface with a fork. Bake at 425° for 15 minutes or until golden brown.

Homemade Noodles / Pasta

Make a well in the flour and add liquids. Pull flour toward center, form dough and knead.

Dough should be rolled out thinly.

Use a rolling cutter for noodles.

Cut noodles are ready to cook.

Noodle Notes:

Mexican Bread

1 - 16 ounce can creamed corn
3/4 cups milk
1/3 cup butter, melted
2 eggs slightly beaten
1 cup corn meal
1/2 teaspoon baking soda
1-4 ounce can green chilies
1-2/3 cups shredded cheddar cheese
1 small can black olives, sliced

Mix all ingredients except chilies and cheese in order given. Pour 1/2 batter into greased 9" pan. Spread with chilies and 1/2 of cheese. Spread remaining batter and cheese. Bake at 350° for 45 - 60 minutes. Cool to set.

Fresh Pasta

3 cups all purpose flour
5 eggs
1/4 teaspoon salt
1 teaspoon vegetable oil

Place flour in a mound in center of large bowl. Make a well in center of flour; add remaining ingredients. Mix thoroughly with fork bringing flour to center until dough forms. (If dough is dry add a few drops of water; if dough is too sticky, add flour.) Knead on lightly floured **No Mess Dough Disc** for 15 minutes or until smooth. Divide dough into 4 equal parts. Roll each part into a rectangle 1/8" to 1/16" thick. Sprinkle dough lightly with flour and cut crosswise into 1/4" strips for fettuccine, 1/8" strips for linguine. Shake out strips. Arrange pasta in a single layer on lightly floured towels or hang to dry on a pasta drying rack. Let stand uncovered for 30 minutes. Cook immediately in boiling water or refrigerate up to 2 days.

Cooking Fresh Pasta

Heat 4 quarts of water to boiling, add pasta. Boil uncovered for 2 - 5 minutes until tender but firm. Do not rinse.

Chili Shrimp Quiche

Pastry:

1 cup all purpose flour
1/8 teaspoon salt
2 tablespoons butter or margarine
2 tablespoons shortening
2 - 4 teaspoons water

Filling:

4 eggs
1/2 cup milk
1/2 cup light cream
1/2 clove garlic, crushed
1 cup cheddar cheese, grated
3 green onions, chopped
2 green chilies, seeded and chopped
8 ounces cooked and peeled shrimp
salt (to taste)

To prepare crust: Sift the flour and salt; cut in shortening and butter until the mixture resembles corn meal. Gradually mix in the liquid adding enough to bring the pastry together. Wrap the pastry and chill for 20 - 30 minutes. Roll out pastry on well floured **No Mess Dough Disc.** Place pastry into 10" flan dish, taking care not to stretch it. Remove excess pastry with rolling pin or knife; flute as desired.

To prepare filling: Mix eggs, milk, cream and garlic together. Sprinkle with cheese, onion, chilies and shrimp. Pour into pastry lined pan. Bake at 400° for 30 - 40 minutes until firm and golden brown.

Jewish Potato Knishes

6 tablespoons shortening
2 onions, chopped
4 cups mashed potatoes (no liquid added)
3 eggs
3/4 cups sifted flour
1 teaspoon salt
1/2 teaspoon pepper
2 tablespoons grated onion

Melt 4 tablespoons of shortening in a skillet. Add chopped onions. Sauté for 10 minutes, stirring frequently. Remove the onions and cool. Pre-heat oven to 375°. Melt the remaining shortening in skillet. Mix together the potatoes, eggs, flour, salt, pepper, grated onions and melted shortening. Knead on lightly floured **No Mess Dough Disc** until smooth. Break off pieces and shape into 2" balls. Make a depression in the center of each and fill with a teaspoonful sautéed onions. Cover the filling with dough. Flatten the balls slightly with the palm of hand. Place on greased cookie sheet. Bake at 375° for 25 minutes or until brown.

Ramekin Au Gruyère

These tasty little treats are perfect party appetizers. Make ahead of time and freeze for easy preparation.

Favorite Pie Dough
4 cups bacon, fried and chopped
4 cups Gruyère cheese
12 eggs, whole
3 egg yolks
3 cups milk
3 cups heavy cream
1 cup Parmesan cheese, grated
3 tablespoons butter, melted
salt, pepper, nutmeg to taste

Line 10 miniature muffin tins with pie dough. (Roll out on **No Mess Dough Disc** and cut into circles to fit muffin tins.) Bake at 400° for 5 minutes until half done. Place bacon and Gruyère cheese evenly in tins. Mix remaining ingredients and pour into muffin tins. Bake at 425° for 15 minutes or until done. Serve immediately. Yield: 10 dozen.

Special Thick Pizza Crust

3 cups of flour
1 teaspoon salt
2-1/2 teaspoons yeast
1 cup warm water (105°)
1/4 cup sugar
1/4 cup honey

Combine yeast, sugar, honey and water; stir to dissolve. Allow the yeast mixture to sit for 5 - 10 minutes until foamy. Add yeast to flour mixture; stir to blend ingredients. Knead on lightly floured **No Mess Dough Disc** for 5 minutes until soft and smooth. Place the dough in a large bowl and cover with damp cloth. Allow the dough to rise for 2 - 3 hours. When ready to make pizza, knead dough on **No Mess Dough Disc** and form the pizza crust. Bake at 475° for 12 - 15 minutes.

Easy Pizza Crust

1 cup warm water
1 package yeast
2 tablespoons oil

Mix in order and set aside.
In a separate bowl combine:

1 teaspoon sugar
1 teaspoon salt
2-1/2 cups all purpose flour

Mix dry ingredients into liquids and beat for 20 strokes. Let stand for 5 minutes. Roll out on lightly floured **No Mess Dough Disc,** transfer to pizza pan. Top with your favorite ingredients. Bake at 475° for 10 - 12 minutes.

Ham and Mushroom Breakfast Pizza

Pizza Crust:

1 cup warm water
1 package yeast
2 tablespoons oil
Mix together and set aside.

2-1/2 cups all purpose flour
1 teaspoon salt
1 teaspoon sugar
1/2 teaspoon poppy seed

Mix flour, salt, sugar and poppy seeds with yeast mixture. Beat for 20 strokes and let stand for 5 minutes. Roll out on **No Mess Dough Disc** and transfer to pizza pan.

Topping:

1 package (4 oz.) sliced cooked ham
1 package (6 oz.) sliced Swiss cheese
1/4 pound mushrooms, sliced
3 green onions, chopped
2 tablespoons butter or margarine
3 eggs
3/4 cups milk

Prepare pastry. Bake pastry crust 5 minutes on lowest rack of pre-heated 425° oven. Gently press down bubbles. Top with ham and cheese. Saute mushrooms and onions in butter until limp. Spread over ham and cheese. Beat eggs and milk; pour over pizza. Return to oven and bake 18 to 20 minutes longer.

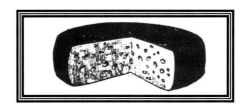

Cheese Brambles

1/2 cup butter
1, 3-oz. package cream cheese
1 cup flour
1/4 teaspoon salt
dash of cayenne pepper
American cheese, cubed

Blend butter and cream cheese together. Add flour, salt and cayenne pepper. Chill. Roll out to 1/8" thickness on **No Mess Dough Disc.** Cut into 2" rounds. Place cheese cubes on half of each round and fold, crimping edges to seal. Place on baking sheet and keep chilled until ready to bake. Bake at 450° for 8 - 10 minutes. Yield: 36 - 40.

German Potato Dumplings

Traditional potato dumplings are a wonderful addition to soups and stews or make a tasty side dish with drizzled butter and chopped parsley or spring onions.

Mix:

6 medium potatoes
3/4 cups flour
1/2 cup bread crumbs
1/4 teaspoon nutmeg
2 teaspoons salt
2 eggs, beaten

Boil unpeeled potatoes; remove skins and let cool. Process potatoes to a coarse mealy texture. Spread on wax paper to dry. Mix dry ingredients; add eggs and make a well in center of mixture. Add potatoes to well and work into flour mixture creating a dough. Place on lightly floured **No Mess Dough Disc** and knead. Pinch off small portions about the size of walnuts, shape into balls and drop into boiling salted water or broth. After dumplings rise to the surface, boil 3 more minutes.

Swedish Tea Ring

1 cake of yeast
1/4 cup sugar
1 cup milk, scalded
2 tablespoons butter
3/4 teaspoons salt
1 egg beaten
2-1/2 cups flour
1/4 cup butter, softened
1/2 cup brown sugar
1 teaspoon cinnamon
1/4 cup nuts, chopped
1/4 cup raisins, optional

Crumble yeast in sugar and let stand until liquefied. Scald milk; add butter and salt. Cool to lukewarm add yeast mixture and egg. Stir in flour to make a soft dough. Knead on lightly floured **No Mess Dough Disc**. Knead dough until smooth and elastic. Place in greased bowl and let rise until double in bulk. Punch down; cover and let rise again, 10 minutes. Roll out to a rectangle 1/2" thick. Brush with soft butter, sprinkle with cinnamon, brown sugar, chopped nuts, and raisins. Roll up tightly from wide side. Pinch to seal edges and shape into a ring on a greased baking sheet. With scissors, cut into ring at 1" intervals being careful not to cut through the ring. Twist each section slightly, turning to side. Brush with butter. Cover and let rise until doubled. Bake at 400° for 25 - 20 minutes. Frost while warm with Sugar Icing and sprinkle with chopped nuts.

Sugar Icing:

1 cup sifted Confectioners sugar
1 teaspoon vanilla, almond or rum extract
2 tablespoons milk

Blend together to desired consistency.

Portuguese Sweet Bread

1 package dry yeast
1/4 cup warm water
1/2 cup milk
1/4 cup butter
1/2 cup sugar
1/2 teaspoon salt
2 eggs
2 teaspoons lemon or orange peel
3-1/2 cups flour
1 egg yolk
1 teaspoon milk

Dissolve yeast in warm water. Heat milk and butter until butter melts. Pour into mixing bowl containing sugar, salt and eggs. Cool to lukewarm. Add grated peel and yeast mixture. Gradually beat in flour to make a soft dough. Knead on lightly floured **No Mess Dough Disc.** Place in greased bowl, turn to coat dough, cover and let rise until double in size. Knead again on lightly floured **No Mess Dough Disc** and shape into a flat cake, 9" in diameter. Place in a greased 9" spring form pan or greased baking sheet. Let rise until doubled. Mix egg yolk and milk; brush top of dough. Bake at 325° for 35 - 40 minutes.

Frozen Kolachky

A popular Bohemian recipe which can be varied with your favorite toppings.

1/2 pound of butter
1 small, 8 ounce carton of light cream
2 teaspoons sugar
1 teaspoon nutmeg
3 eggs, (omit one yolk)
1 yeast cake
flour to make a heavy dough
chopped prunes or fruit of your choice

Mix cream and butter; add remaining ingredients. Crumble yeast cake into mixture and add flour to make a heavy dough. Let stand overnight in the refrigerator. Roll out chilled dough to 1/2" thickness on lightly floured **No Mess Dough Disc.** Cut in small circles and place on baking sheet. Top with chopped prunes or other fruit; let stand until raised. Bake at 400° for 15 - 20 minutes.

Jewish Almond Bread

2 eggs, well - beaten
1/2 cup sugar
grated rind of 1 lemon
1 teaspoon lemon juice
1/4 teaspoon vanilla extract
1/4 teaspoon almond extract
pinch of salt
1-2/3 cups flour
1/4 cup oil or soft butter
1/4 cup almonds, blanched and slivered
2 teaspoons baking powder

Beat eggs and sugar until light. Add lemon rind and juice, vanilla, almond extract and 1 cup of flour. Blend well. Add almonds, remaining flour sifted with baking powder and salt. Add oil or butter. Knead on lightly floured **No Mess Dough Disc** until smooth. Shape into 2 long loaves about 1-1/2" thick. Place on greased baking sheet. Bake at 350° for 30 minutes until brown. Cut while warm in 1/2" thick slices.

Cornish Pasty

This savory turnover comes from Cornwall, England, and is a favorite menu item in pubs and cafes.

1-1/2 pounds beef, cut in 1" cubes
1 large onion, cubed
4 medium potatoes, cubed
4 carrots or rutabagas, cubed
1 teaspoon salt
1/4 teaspoon pepper
2 No Fail Pie Crust Pastries (page 6)

Mix beef, vegetables and seasonings. Divide into 4 parts. Roll pastry dough into 4 rounds on lightly floured **No Mess Dough Disc.** Place 1/4 of beef mixture in the center of each round. Pull up pastry from opposite sides, pinch together to seal entire opening. Place on baking sheet. Bake at 350° for 1 hour. Yield: 4 pasties.

Potato Pastry Sausage Rolls

1 cup flour
1/4 cup shortening
1/4 cup diced potatoes
ice water
1/2 pound sausage meat
1 egg white, unbeaten
1/2 teaspoon salt

Sift flour and salt together. Cut in shortening until crumbly. Cut in potatoes; add enough water to bind ingredients. Roll out to 1/8" in thickness on lightly floured **No Mess Dough Disc**. Cut into 3" squares. Form sausage meat into rolls, 3" long. Place meat roll on pastry and roll up tightly. Brush edges with egg white and seal. Place on greased baking dish, seam side down. Make several slices in pastry, brush with egg white. Bake at 350° for 30 - 40 minutes. Yield: 4 - 6.

German Marmalade Rolls

Küchen Orange Rolls

2-1/2 cups milk
4 tablespoons butter
4 tablespoons sugar
1-1/2 teaspoons salt
2 yeast cakes
1/2 cup lukewarm water
5 cups sifted flour
melted butter
orange marmalade

Scald milk; add butter or shortening stirring until melted. Add sugar and salt. Cool. Soften yeast in warm water, add to cooled mixture. Stir in 2-1/2 cups flour; mix well. Cover and let rise 2 hours. Add more flour to make a stiff dough. Knead on lightly floured **No Mess Dough Disc**. Cover and let rise in a warm place until double. Roll out on lightly floured **No Mess Dough Disc;** cut with biscuit cutter. Brush with melted butter and place 1 teaspoon marmalade in center. Fold each in half and place on greased baking sheet. Brush tops with butter. Let stand in a warm place for 30 minutes. Bake at 425° for 20 minutes. Yield: 40 rolls.

German Marmalade Strips

Use same recipe as German Marmalade Rolls

Roll dough out thinly, on lightly floured **No Mess Dough Disc.** Place a layer of dough on inverted baking sheet. Spread thickly with orange marmalade and layer with dough. Cut into strips 4" x 1-1/2." Bake at 425° for 10 minutes. When cooled, spread with Sugar Icing and chopped nuts.

Sugar Icing:

1 cup confectioners sugar
1 tablespoon water

Blend to desired consistency, adding more water if needed.

Pot Stickers

Dough:

3 cups white flour
1-1/2 cups boiling water

Filling:

8 cabbage leaves, Bok Choi or Nappa
Boiling water
1 pound boneless pork shoulder, finely chopped
3 green onions, finely chopped
1 sprig parsley, finely minced
1/2 teaspoon ginger root, minced
2 tablespoons thin soy sauce
1 tablespoon dry sherry
1 tablespoon sesame oil
1 teaspoon sugar
1/2 teaspoon salt
2 - 3 teaspoons corn starch

Sauce:

1/4 cup dark soy sauce
1 tablespoon sesame seed oil
1/2 teaspoon ginger root, minced
1 tablespoon green onion, finely minced

The pastry dough is a 2 to 1 mixture of flour and boiling water. The boiling water cooks the flour and makes a smooth pastry consistency. Combine and mix flour and water until thoroughly blended. Allow to cool, then knead on a well floured **No Mess Dough Disc** about 5 minutes until spongy. Let rest for 30 minutes.

Filling:

Wash and break the cabbage leaves into a large bowl, pour boiling water over to wilt. Drain completely and mince in a food processor. Drain the excess water from cabbage. In second bowl, combine pork, cabbage, green onions and parsley. In another bowl combine remaining ingredients and stir in pork mixture. The filling should have the consistency of lumpy porridge. Add more cornstarch if needed.

Cont.>

Dumplings:

Roll the dough into 1/16" thickness and cut into 3-1/2" circles. Place a circle in the palm of hand and form into a shallow cup. Moisten the outer edges with water. Put 1 teaspoon filling in the center and fold in half. Pinch to seal, forming a half moon. Pleat one side and pinch; working from one end to the other. Place on a floured cookie sheet, pleated side up. Follow the cooking instructions for immediate use or freeze.

Cooking:

Use a very heavy frying pan with lid. Heat to medium high and add 2 tablespoons oil. When oil is moderately hot but not smoking, add dumplings. Arrange snugly but not squeezed together. Brown the bottoms slowly, checking to avoid burning. When bottoms are medium brown, add 1 cup boiling water. The liquids should be absorbed in about 10 minutes. If using frozen dumplings it is not necessary to thaw, but increase steaming time.

Sauce:

Combine all ingredients and use for dipping.

Stir together and serve. Yield: 12 -14 servings.

Polish Potato Dumplings, *Pirogis*

2-1/2 cups flour
1 teaspoon salt
1 egg
1 cup warm water
5 medium potatoes; peeled, boiled and mashed
2/3 cups warm milk
1 tablespoon butter
1-1/2 cups cubed processed cheese
salt and pepper to taste
2 tablespoons butter
1/4 cup onions, chopped
sour cream
bacon bits
chives

Mix first 4 ingredients together to make dough. Roll out on lightly floured **No Mess Dough Disc** and cut into circles 4" - 6" in diameter. Combine mashed potatoes, milk, butter, salt, pepper and cheese. Fill pastry circles with 1/8 - 1/4 cup of potato filling. Pinch edges together and seal with a fork dipped in water. Freeze on cookie sheet then store in plastic bag until ready to use.

To Cook:

Place frozen dumplings in boiling water; the dumplings will sink, then float to the top when cooked. Remove cooked dumplings and drain. Place butter in skillet; add onions and dumplings, cook until brown on all sides. Serve with sour cream and garnish with bacon bits and chives.

Rebecca's Pretzels

2 packages yeast
1-1/2 cups warm water
2 tablespoons sugar
1 teaspoon course salt
4 cups flour
1 egg, beaten

Mix all ingredients except salt and egg. Knead on lightly floured **No Mess Dough Disc** until dough becomes rubbery. Pull off small amounts and roll between hands into different sizes and lengths. Twist into pretzel shapes. Coat with beaten egg then sprinkle with salt. Bake at 425° for 10 - 15 minutes.

German Rolls, *Küchen*

5 egg yolks, beaten
1 large can evaporated milk
1 tablespoon salt
1 stick butter, melted
flour
fat for frying

Mix first 5 ingredients using enough flour to make a stiff dough. Knead on lightly floured **No Mess Dough Disc** and roll out thinly. Cut into 2" x 5" pieces. Drop into deep hot fat. Fry until golden brown. Drain on paper towels. Serve with jelly, jam or honey. Yield: 2-1/2 - 3 dozen.

Pretzel Rolls, German

2-1/4 cups bread flour
1 package quick rising yeast
1 teaspoon salt
1 teaspoon sugar
1 teaspoon celery seeds
1 cup plus 2 tablespoons hot water (125° to 130°)
corn meal
8 cups water
1/4 cup baking soda
2 tablespoons sugar
1 egg white, beaten
coarse salt

Combine bread flour, yeast, salt, sugar and celery seeds in food processor and blend. With machine running, gradually, add hot water through feed tube until a smooth, elastic dough is formed. Process 1 minute to knead. Grease medium bowl; add dough, turn to coat cover with plastic wrap and let rise until doubled, about 35 minutes. Divide dough into 8 pieces. Form each dough piece into a ball. Place dough balls on prepared sheet, flattening each slightly. Make an "X" on the tops with a serrated knife. Cover with towel and let rise until almost double; 20 minutes. Preheat oven to 375°. Grease another baking sheet and sprinkle with cornmeal. Bring 8 cups of water to boil in a large saucepan. Add baking soda and 2 tablespoons sugar (water will foam). Add 4 rolls to boiling water and cook for 30 seconds per side. Using a slotted spoon, transfer to prepared baking sheet. Repeat with remaining rolls. Brush rolls with egg white glaze. Sprinkle generously with coarse salt. Bake at 375° for 25 minutes or until brown. Transfer to racks and cool.

German Marmalade Cake

2 packages dry yeast
1/4 cup warm water
1/4 cup sugar
1 teaspoon salt
1/2 cup shortening
1 cup hot milk
4 - 5 cups enriched flour
2 eggs
Any flavor of jam, jelly or marmalade
2 tablespoons butter, softened

Soften yeast in warm water 5 minutes. Stir well. In a large bowl add sugar, shortening, salt and hot milk. Mix well. Cool to luke-warm. Stir in 2 cups of flour to make a thick batter, beat 100 strokes. Add yeast and eggs; stir until blended. Mix 1-1/2 cups - 2 cups of flour to make a dough that does not stick to fingers. Knead on lightly floured **No Mess Dough Disc** for 2 minutes. Place dough in greased bowl, turn to coat dough, cover and let rise until double in bulk 1-1/2 hours. Punch down. Place on floured **No Mess Dough Disc** and roll into a 9" circle. Put dough in a greased 9" cake pan, cover and let rise until double in bulk, 45 minutes. With handle of wooden spoon make deep holes in the surface 2" apart. Dot each hole with butter and fill with your favorite, jam, jelly or marmalade. Bake at 375° for 20 - 30 minutes. Serve hot with Apricot Sauce.

Apricot Sauce:

3/4 cups sugar
1-1/2 cup apricot juice
2 teaspoons lemon juice

Boil suger and apricot juice rapidly for 5 minutes. Remove from heat and add lemon juice. Apricot Rum Sauce: Add 1/2 cup of dark rum to Apricot Sauce.

Top right, clockwise: Peach Pie, Arkansas Cornbread, Syble's Biscuits, Chicken with Dressing, Ham with Red Eye Gravy, Chicken & Dumplings.

Apple Dumplings

Dough:

1 cup shortening
3 cups flour
1 teaspoon salt
1 egg, beaten
1 tablespoon vinegar
5 tablespoons water

Filling:

5 - 6 medium apples, peeled and sliced
1 tablespoon butter or margarine
2 tablespoons cinnamon sugar to each square of dough

Syrup:

2-1/2 cups sugar
1-1/4 cups water
1-1/2 cubes butter or margarine
nutmeg

Cut together shortening, flour, and salt. Mix egg, vinegar, water; stir into flour mixture. Form a ball; divide and roll dough on floured **No Mess Dough Disc**. Cut dough into 10 squares, add sliced apples to dough, plus 1 tablespoon margarine and 2 tablespoons of cinnamon sugar. Fold over dough or bring corners together and pinch. Bake 30 minutes at 350°. Cook syrup until dissolved. Pour around dumplings and bake 15 - 20 minutes longer.

Variation:

Core a whole apple and fill with nuts or raisins, butter and spice mixture. Wrap with dough square and bake according to recipe.

Red Onion Rings

1 large red onion, cut in 1/2" thick rounds
2 cups buttermilk
1-1/2 teaspoons ground cumin
vegetable oil for frying
3/4 cups flour
1/4 cup corn meal
1 teaspoon salt
1 teaspoon pepper

Separate onions into rings. Combine onions, buttermilk and 1 teaspoon cumin in large bowl. Let soak for 1 hour, stirring occasionally. Pour oil into large saucepan for frying. Heat oil to 375°. Mix flour, corn meal, salt, pepper and remaining cumin in a cake pan. Place onion rings, a few at a time in flour mixture and coat. Fry in hot oil, drain and season with salt and pepper if desired.

Fried Corn

8 ears of fresh corn
3 tablespoons butter
1 teaspoon sugar
salt & pepper to taste

Cut corn off cob. Scrape cob thoroughly. Melt butter in non-stick pan over medium heat. Add corn and sugar. Stir frequently for 10 - 15 minutes over medium heat. Salt and pepper to taste. Serves 6.

Fried Green Tomatoes

3 - 4 medium green tomatoes
1 egg, beaten
1/8 cup milk
1/2 cup flour
1/2 cup corn meal
salt & pepper to taste

Slice tomatoes to 1/8" - 1/4" thick. In a small bowl beat egg and milk. In a small flat dish or pan combine flour and corn meal. Dip sliced tomatoes in egg mixture then roll in flour and corn meal. Salt to taste. Deep fry in enough hot oil to cover tomatoes.

Variation:

2 cups of sliced okra is also quite delicious prepared in this manner.

Southern Style Dumplings

Add broth to flour mixture for authentic southern style dumplings.

Dough should be thick and elastic.

Cut dumplings into squares using the back of a butter knife.

Use No Mess Dough Disc to hold dumplings in place while dropping into broth.

Southern Roll Dumplings

1 cup flour
1-1/2 teaspoon baking powder
1/2 teaspoon salt
1-1/2 tablespoon shortening
1/2 cup milk

Sift together flour, baking powder and salt. Sift again and cut in shortening; add milk and stir until thick. Empty contents onto floured **No Mess Dough Disc** and roll out like pie dough to 1/4" thickness. Cut into 2" - 3" squares and drop into boiling broth. Cover tightly and cook on low heat 20 minutes without removing cover. *Do not boil over.*

Egg Noodles

1/2 cup flour
1/4 teaspoon salt
1 egg
1/8 cup milk or water

Mix all ingredients together with fork, adding more flour to make a stiff dough. Roll out on floured **No Mess Dough Disc** until very thin. Cut into strips and let dry at least one hour. Boil rapidly in salted water or broth.

Never - Fail Noodles

Flour
2 egg yolks, slightly beaten
1 tablespoon shortening
2 tablespoon whipping cream
1/4 teaspoon baking powder
1/4 teaspoon salt

Mix all ingredients together with enough flour to make a stiff dough. Roll out on floured **No Mess Dough Disc** and cut in strips. Cook in boiling broth. It is not necessary to dry these noodles before cooking.

Plain Homemade Noodles

1 cup flour
2 eggs
1 teaspoon salt

Mix ingredients well. Knead on lightly floured **No Mess Dough Disc,** adding flour if needed. Allow to rest for 30 minutes. Roll out as thinly as desired on lightly floured **No Mess Dough Disc** and let dry 1 - 2 hours. Cut into fine strips. For easier cutting, cut 2" - 3" strips, layer in a stack and cut to narrower width.

Barb's Fried Chicken

4 - 6 pieces of skinless chicken
3/4 - 1 cup flour
1 teaspoon Greek Seasoning
salt and pepper
shortening or oil for frying

Wash chicken well and remove skin. Drain. Mix flour, seasoning, salt and pepper in a bowl or bag. Heat shortening over high heat. Place coated chicken in skillet, cover. Turn heat to medium to prevent burning. Let brown evenly on both sides. Cook for 35 - 40 minutes. For crispy chicken, take the lid off every 2 minutes and turn the chicken until done. For tender chicken, leave lid on half way and turn heat to low. Drain on paper towels and serve.

Marlene's Spicy Fried Chicken

2-1/2 - 3 pounds chicken parts, cut up
1-1/4 cups all purpose flour
2 teaspoons salt
1 teaspoon pepper
1 teaspoon ground sage
1/2 teaspoon onion powder
1/2 teaspoon crushed thyme
1/2 teaspoon garlic powder
2 eggs
2 tablespoons water
oil for frying

Rinse chicken and pat dry. In a large bowl combine flour and seasoning. In second bowl combine eggs and water. Place chicken (a few pieces at a time) in plastic bag with flour mixture, shake to coat. Place coated chicken in egg mixture, drain slightly and coat again in flour mixture. Fill skillet with oil about 1". Heat oil for frying and place chicken in skillet, skin side down. Cook for 10 -12 minutes. Turn and fry for 10 - 15 minutes longer or until golden brown and thoroughly cooked.

Cocoa Gravy

Ask anyone in the Wood household about their favorite biscuit topping and they all agree it's Cocoa Gravy; it's not a dessert but a delicious variation to traditional white gravy.

1/4 cup oil
1/4 cup flour
1/8 cup cocoa
1/2 cup sugar
2 cups milk
1 teaspoon vanilla

Mix cocoa and sugar together in a small bowl. Set aside. Heat oil in medium sized skillet, add flour to oil, and stir. Add cocoa and sugar mixture. Pour in milk cook over medium heat until desired thickness. Add vanilla, stir to blend and serve.

Sherried Ham

Dough:

1-3/4 cups sifted flour
1/2 teaspoon celery salt
5 tablespoons butter
1/3 - 1/2 cup cold apple juice or sherry

Blend flour and salt; work in butter until dough is mealy. Add enough apple juice to moisten flour so it hold its shape when pressed into a ball. Roll out on lightly floured **No Mess Dough Disc** to a 10" circle. Line an 8" cake pan and refrigerate until ready to fill.

Filling:

3 eggs
1-1/2 cups heavy cream
1 teaspoon salt
1/8 teaspoon pepper
1/8 teaspoon mace
2/3 cups diced ham

Mix eggs, cream, salt, pepper and mace. Sprinkle diced ham in bottom of pan. Pour egg mixture over meat. Cut away excess dough from edges, flute. Bake at 375° for 40 minutes. Serves: 6.

Stove Top Juicy Roast

2 - 3 pounds roast beef or beef stew chunks
3 - 4 medium potatoes
2- 3 carrots optional
1 - 2 teaspoons onion powder
salt and pepper

Rinse roast with water. In a large skillet grease bottom and sides to prevent sticking. Place roast in warm skillet to brown on each side. Pour enough water to simmer meat. Add onion powder, salt and pepper. Let simmer on medium heat. Cover and cook for 2 hours. Check for doneness. Peel and quarter potatoes; peel and cut carrots into 2" lengths; add to roast. Cover and simmer for 1 hour until vegetables are tender. Remove roast and vegetables from juice. Make gravy, slice and serve. If using stew meat, reduce cooking time to 1-1/2 hours.

Gravy:

2 teaspoons cornstarch
1/2 package of brown gravy mix
1 cup cold water

Mix cornstarch, gravy mix and water. Add to boiling juice in skillet and stir until thickened. Remove from heat and adjust to desired thickness.

Southern - Style Chicken & Dumplings

The family secret is adding chicken broth to the dumpling dough; it adds richness and flavor to the sauce.

4 cups all purpose flour
1 tablespoon salt
1-1/2 sticks of butter or margarine
2 cups boiling chicken broth
1 whole chicken, cut up

Boil chicken in large pot until done. Remove chicken and continue to boil broth. Mix flour and salt; add butter or margarine. Strain 2 cups of boiling broth. Pour over flour and butter mixture. (No need to blend butter and flour, just pour broth directly over mixture.) Mix until dough leaves sides of bowl. Generously flour **No Mess Dough Disc** and roll out to 1/8" thickness using between a quarter and third of the dough at a time. Cut into 3" squares and drop into boiling broth. After all dumplings are submerged, simmer for 15- 20 minutes, stirring occasionally. Add chicken meat to dumplings and broth.

Country Ham and Red - Eye Gravy

The strong, sweet taste of coffee is a wonderful compliment to the naturally salty taste of ham.

4 slices country ham, sliced 1/4" thick
1 cup strong coffee

Trim excess fat from ham. Rub the bottom of a heavy cast - iron skillet with enough ham fat to grease it thoroughly. Heat the skillet until it is very hot. Add ham slices and brown on both sides. Pour the coffee into the skillet. Bring to a boil and simmer for 7 minutes or until ham is tender. Serve immediately with hot biscuits.

Tangy Ham Roll Ups

1-1/2 cups flour
1-1/2 teaspoons baking powder
1/2 teaspoon salt
1 cup Cheddar cheese, shredded
1/2 cup butter
1/4 cup cold water
8 thin slices boiled ham
*mustard optional

Sift flour, baking powder and salt in bowl. Combine with cheese and butter. Gradually add water, stirring with fork until dough sticks together. Knead 10 times on lightly floured **No Mess Dough Disc.** Divide dough in half. Roll out each half to 10" x 12" rectangle. Cut each rectangle into 4, 5" x 6" pieces. Place ham slice on each piece of dough. Spread lightly with mustard. Roll up like jelly roll from narrow end. Pinch to seal edges. Place seam side down on greased cookie sheet. Bake at 450° for 10 - 12 minutes. Cut each roll into 5 or 6 slices. Serve while hot. Serves 8 - 10.

100

Chicken Pie

2 tablespoons butter
1/2 cup celery, chopped
1 cup onions, diced
1 cup tomatoes, diced
3 tablespoons flour
1 teaspoon seasoned salt
2 cups mashed potatoes
2 cups chicken, cooked and cut in pieces
1-1/2 cups chicken stock
3 tablespoons oil
9" pie shell, unbaked
parsley
paprika

In large skillet, melt butter. Add celery and onions and simmer 2 - 3 minutes. Add chicken and cook until thoroughly heated. Add tomatoes. Combine flour and oil and add to stock to thicken. Stir into chicken mixture. Add salt and simmer 10 minutes. Pour into pie shell and spread with mashed potatoes. Sprinkle with parsley and paprika. Bake at 350° for 1 hour. Serves 4 to 6.

Potato Broccoli Cheddar Cheese Pie

3 oz. cheddar cheese
9" pie shell, unbaked
1 medium potato, boiled without skin
1-10 oz. package frozen broccoli, chopped and thawed
1/2 cup skim milk
2 large eggs
2 tablespoons all-purpose flour
3/4 teaspoon salt
1/8 teaspoon pepper
1/8 teaspoon nutmeg

Preheat oven to 350°. Shred cheese and sprinkle 1 oz. into unbaked pie shell. Bake for 5 minutes. Remove from oven. Shred potato; mix in broccoli and combine with remaining ingredients. Stir to combine and pour into pie shell. Place on baking sheet. Bake at 350° for 1 hour or until done.

Wood Family's Favorite Pinto Beans

1 package dried pinto beans
1 teaspoon baking soda
3 - 4 ham hocks
salt to taste
water

Prepare and clean beans according to package directions. Cover beans in a large pot with water and baking soda. Soak overnight. Drain water, cover with 2 quarts of fresh water. Bring to a boil, cover reduce heat to low. Check every 30 minutes, stir and add water if needed. After 1-1/2 hours of cooking add ham hocks. Cook 2 - 2-1/2 hours or until beans are very tender. To thicken bean juice turn heat to high for 20 - 30 minutes stirring every 5 minutes. Remove from heat, salt to taste and serve.

Southern Wilted Salad

This recipe is great with corn bread and pinto beans.

1 small bundle leaf lettuce
1/2 cup sliced green onions
1/2 cup sliced red or white radishes
dash of pepper
4 - 6 slices of cooked bacon, diced (reserve bacon drippings)

Break lettuce into small pieces; add onions, radishes and a dash of pepper. Toss. Fry bacon until crisp, remove and crumble into small pieces. Add to salad. Pour very hot bacon drippings over salad. Eat immediately. Serves 4.

Country Corn Pudding

1 can creamed corn
2 eggs, beaten
3/4 cups milk
1 tablespoon butter
1 tablespoon flour
1 tablespoon pimento, finely chopped
1 tablespoon onion, finely chopped
1 tablespoon green pepper, finely chopped
1/2 teaspoon salt
3/4 teaspoons celery salt
1 teaspoon sugar
2 teaspoons lemon juice

Melt butter, blend in flour, add milk. Stir constantly until sauce boils and thickens. Add remaining ingredients (except eggs) and re-heat. Stir hot mixture into well beaten eggs. Mix well. Pour into buttered 9" x 12" baking dish. Bake at 350° for 1 hour or until sharp knife inserted into center comes out clean.

Arkansas Hot Water Corn Bread

2 cups white corn meal
boiling water
1/2 cup buttermilk
1/4 teaspoon salt
1/4 teaspoon baking soda

Mix corn meal with enough boiling water to make a stiff mush or dough. Add buttermilk, salt and baking soda. Mix well. Form dough into small patties and fry in hot shortening for about 10 minutes. Turn 2 - 3 times during cooking. Serves 4.

Arkansas Spoon Bread

1 cup white corn meal
1-1/2 teaspoons salt
4 tablespoons margarine
1-1/3 cups boiling water
3 eggs
1 tablespoon baking powder
1-1/3 cups hot milk
2 tablespoons honey

Pre-heat oven to 350°. Grease 2-quart casserole. Mix corn meal and salt. Add margarine, pour in boiling water, stirring constantly. Allow to cool. Beat eggs with baking powder until light and fluffy. Add to corn meal mixture. Stir in milk and honey. Mix thoroughly. Pour into greased casserole. Place in shallow pan of hot water. Bake at 350° for 35 - 40 minutes.

Corn Bread

2-1/2 cups corn meal
1 cup flour
2 tablespoons baking powder
1 teaspoon salt
1/4 cup shortening
2 large eggs
1-1/2 cups milk

Mix dry ingredients thoroughly. Add shortening; blend with dry ingredients. Add eggs and milk, beat for 1 minute. Place in a greased 12" pan. Bake at 425° for 20 - 25 minutes.

Turkey or Chicken Dressing

Don't wait until Thanksgiving to try this delicious recipe.

5 cups corn bread, crumbled
1 cup bread crumbs
1/2 cup onion, diced
1/2 cup celery, diced
1/4 cup butter
1-1/2 teaspoons sage or to taste
1 teaspoon salt
1 teaspoon pepper
3 -1/2 cups chicken or turkey broth
3 large eggs
1 cup chicken or turkey meat

Saute diced onions and celery in butter. Mix dry ingredients thoroughly. Add sauted onions, celery, liquid and poultry meat, blend together. Place dressing around chicken or turkey in greased baking dish. Bake at 400° for 30 minutes.

Southern Style Strawberry Shortcake

The traditional version made with strawberries can be modified with any fresh berries or peaches, so there's no excuse not to serve this easy to make dessert all year long!

1-3/4 cups unsifted, plain flour
3 teaspoons baking powder
3/4 teaspoons salt
1/4 cup sugar
1/2 cup shortening
1/4 cup milk
1 egg, well beaten

Mix flour, baking powder, salt and sugar together. Cut in shortening, until mixture resembles coarse meal, using pastry blender or fork. Add milk and egg. Stir with fork until soft dough is formed. Knead on lightly floured **No Mess Dough Disc** about 30 seconds. Roll to 1/4" thickness. Cut with floured 3" cutter. Place half the circles on baking sheet; brush with melted butter. Place remaining circles on top; brush with butter. Bake at 425° for 10 -12 minutes.

To Serve:

Separate the hot shortcakes, spread with softened butter. Spoon chilled strawberries onto bottom layer, top with whipped cream, add top shortcake layer and garnish with whipped cream.

Variation:

Grated orange rind may be added to dough for more fruit flavor.

Norene's Fried Pies

Filling:

2 (16 ounce) packages dried apricots
3 cups water
1/2 cup cornstarch
1 cup sugar

Cook apricots in water about 30 minutes or until softened. Mix cornstarch and sugar together and add to cooked apricots. Stir to thicken. Set aside until crust is ready.

Crust:

3 cups flour
1/2 cup shortening
1 egg
1 cup water
1 tablespoon salt

Mix ingredients together. Roll dough to 1/4" on floured **No Mess Dough Disc** and cut into 6" rounds or desired size. Place 2 table-spoons of apricot mixture in center of each round. Fold over, press edges together and crimp with a fork to seal. Deep fry in hot oil. Drain on paper towels.

Ozark Pumpkin Roll

3 eggs
1 cup sugar
1 teaspoon ginger
1/2 teaspoon nutmeg
1 teaspoon soda
1/2 teaspoon salt
3/4 cups flour
2/3 cups canned pumpkin
1 cup walnuts, coarsely chopped
1/2 cup powdered sugar (for dusting tea towel)

Mix all ingredients except nuts and powdered sugar together to make a batter. Pour into well greased jellyroll pan. Sprinkle with nuts and bake at 375° for 15 - 20 minutes. Do not over - bake! Dust a tea towel with powdered sugar and invert baked pumpkin roll onto towel while cake is warm. Roll up tightly with towel and allow to cool. Unroll cooled pumpkin roll and spread with filling. Roll up tightly (without towel) and allow to set. Slice into 1" sections and serve.

Filling

1 - 8 ounce package cream cheese, softened
4 tablespoons margarine
1 cup powdered sugar
1 teaspoon vanilla

Four - In - One Ice Cream Soda

4 kids
4 straws
4 spoons
1 quart of ice cream
1 pint soda pop
1 large bowl
whipped cream

Place ice cream and soda in a large bowl. Top with a large serving of whipped cream. Gather four kids around and give each a spoon and straw and let them "dig in".

Something for the Kids - Playdough

1 cup flour
1/2 cup salt
2 teaspoons cream of tartar
1 tablespoon cooking oil
1 cup water
food coloring

Mix the dry ingredients. Add oil and water; mix well. Cook over medium heat, 3 - 5 minutes, or until mixture pulls away from sides of pan. Remove from heat, allow to cool and knead on **No Mess Dough Disc** until smooth. Divide into 4 parts; add food coloring until desired color is obtained. Store in airtight containers.

Sun Kissed Children

Take

1 large field or pasture
half a dozen children
2 or 3 small dogs
a pinch of a brook or creek
and some pebbles or stones

Mix the children and the dogs well; put them on the field, stirring constantly. Pour the brook over the pebbles; sprinkle the field with flowers; spread over all a deep blue sky and bake in the sun. When brown, set away to cool in the bathtub.

INDEX

Q

R

S